"*Stamp Album* paints a picture of hitherto unknown 'catacomb Russia'. The communal apartment Sergeev describes is not a typical community of Soviet citizens... They neither fight the regime, nor adapt to it... Sergeev's memory seems to collect mere trifles: children's ditties, counting rhymes, old slogans, newspaper clippings, snatches of conversations, official documents, urban folklore and much else. He fishes various fragments out of this detritus and files them carefully away in his stamp album." — Natalia Pervukhina in *Russkaya Mysl*

"Sergeev's extraordinary memory, the skill of a professional collector, his fantastic sharpness of vision, his passion for details and objects as well as for individuals — all these make *Stamp Album* fascinating reading." — *The Russian Journal*

"The author of this text-collage is clearly a passionate collector of all sorts of things: coins, stamps, period objects, interesting people, curious words, and anecdotes. *Stamp Album* is a memoir composed of verbal photographs." — *Ex Libris*

"A true master of time, Sergeev will always be absolutely contemporary. He stands alone..." — Alexander Pyatigorsky in *Novoye Literaturnoye Obozreniye*

"I value Sergeev's opinion exceedingly. I would even say that Sergeev's opinion of my poems has always been more important to me than anything on earth: If there existed some higher or last judgment for me in matters of poetry, then it was Sergeev's opinion." — Joseph Brodsky

Other books in the Glas series

(more than 100 authors featured)

REVOLUTION, the 1920s and 1980s
SOVIET GROTESQUE, young people's rebellion
WOMEN'S VIEW, Russian woman bloodied but unbowed
LOVE AND FEAR, the two strongest emotions dominating Russian life
BULGAKOV & MANDELSTAM, earlier autobiographical stories
JEWS & STRANGERS, what it means to be a Jew in Russia
BOOKER WINNERS & OTHERS, mostly provincial writers
LOVE RUSSIAN STYLE, Russia tries decadence
THE SCARED GENERATION, the grim background of today's ruling class
BOOKER WINNERS & OTHERS-II, more Booker winners
CAPTIVES, victors turn out to be captives on conquered territory
FROM THREE WORLDS, new Ukrainian writing
A WILL & A WAY, new women's writing
BEYOND THE LOOKING-GLAS, Russian grotesque revisited
CHILDHOOD, the child is father to the man

Peter Aleshkovsky, *Skunk A Life,* a novel set in the Russian countryside
Ludmila Ulitskaya, *Sonechka,* a novel about a persevering woman
Asar Eppel, *The Grassy Street,* a Moscow suburb in the 1940s
Boris Slutsky, *Things That Happened,* the poetry & biography
THE PORTABLE PLATONOV, for the centenary of Russia's greatest writer
Leonid Latynin, *The Face-Maker and the Muse,* a novel-parable
Irina Muravyova, *The Nomadic Soul,* a novel about a modern Anna Karenina
Anatoly Mariengof, *A Novel Without Lies,* Bohemian Moscow in the 1920s
Alexander Genis, *Red Bread,* Russian and US civilizations compared
Larissa Miller, *Dim and Distant Days,* childhood in postwar Moscow
Andrei Volos, *Hurramabad,* Tajik national strife after the collapse of the USSR
Lev Rubinstein, *Here I Am,* performance poems and essays
Valery Ronshin, *Living a Life, Absurd Tales*

ANDREI SERGEEV

Stamp Album

A Collection
of People,
Things,
Relationships
and Words

Translated by Joanne Turnbull

glas

GLAS NEW RUSSIAN WRITING

contemporary Russian literature in English translation

The Editors of the Glas series
Natasha Perova & Arch Tait & Joanne Turnbull

Volume 28

Cover design by Eric Pervukhin
Camera-ready copy: Tatiana Shaposhnikova

GLAS Publishers
tel./fax: +7(095)441 9157
e-mail: perova@glas.msk.su

www.russianpress.com/glas
www.russianwriting.com

As of 2002, Glas is distributed in North America by
NORTHWESTERN UNIVERSITY PRESS.
Chicago Distribution Center, 11030 South Langley Avenue
Chicago, IL 60628, USA
tel: 1-800-621-2736 or 773-568-1550
fax: 1-800-621-8476 or 773-660-2235

ISBN 5-7172-0059-5

Printed at the 'Nauka' printing press, Moscow

CONTENTS

FOREWORD

Stamp Album — despite winning the Russian Booker Prize — is not a novel, but a novel memoir. A collector of stamps from childhood, the poet and writer Andrei Sergeev (1933-98) later collected impressions as well, impressions of people, things, relationships and words, here displayed as lovingly yet frankly as coins — another lifelong passion — in glass cases.

During his lifetime, Sergeev was better known as a distinguished translator of English poetry, including that of T.S. Eliot, Robert Frost and W.H. Auden. In the 1950s he belonged to an underground literary group that was among the first to use samizdat (hand-production and dissemination of banned books). In the 1960s he became a friend of Joseph Brodsky, who dedicated a major poem to Sergeev. But it wasn't until the 1990's that Sergeev's own poems and autobiographical prose — lapidary in style and full of evocative detail — began to appear in Russian literary journals.

In *Stamp Album*, Sergeev draws on his extraordinary store of personal recollections as well as on old letters, photographs, family documents, Soviet slogans, street conversations, popular songs, children's rhymes and irreverences to recreate the very texture and perversity of Soviet life in the 1930s, '40s and '50s. *Stamp Album* is, if you will, Sergeev's *Speak, Memory*. But whereas Nabokov's memory speaks in complete sentences and long descriptive paragraphs, Sergeev's can be as elliptical and cryptic as the actual scenes it reproduces. *Stamp Album* is straight memory — with nary a word of retroactive explanation added for the reader's benefit. Thus the reader comes at Sergeev's life as he did himself at the time — particularly in childhood and adolescence.

The first three chapters ('Before the War', 'The War', and 'The Communal Apartment') slip back and forth between the *kommunalka* in Moscow where Sergeev grew up (the best room is occupied by the eccentric widow of a French merchant, an erstwhile prostitute now bedridden with gout to whom the entire apartment belonged before the Revolution) and the dacha in Udelnaya where he spent his summers and where this collage of verbal snapshots begins ("I'm lying on Mama's trestle bed... A small gland in my neck has become inflamed. The stately surgeon bicycles over from Malakhovka...").

The fourth chapter, 'Father', takes Yakov Sergeev from the village of Zhukovka, where he was born, through military service in the tsarist army to Moscow where he taught at the Timiryazev Agricultural Academy and married Andrei's colorful and capricious mother.

The fifth and final chapter, 'Bolshaya Ekaterininskaya', takes its name from the ramshackle Moscow street where Sergeev's maternal grandmother (the daughter of a wet nurse to a merchant family) and grandfather (a peasant orphan who came to the city as an apprentice at the age of eight) lived all their married life. It is a rare and amazingly comprehensive portrait of a lower middle class enclave from pre-revolutionary times to the 1950s.

Sergeev's extended family mostly eluded Stalin's murderous machinery. Survivors, they came to see the Revolution as a defeat but, like so many others, stifled any objections to what they could not change. They belonged to the vast and little known recesses of what Sergeev called 'catacomb Russia'.

Sergeev began writing and assembling *Stamp Album* (for the drawer) in the 1970s, completing the manuscript only fifteen years later. To Sergeev, the most important aspect of literature was not invention but truth. *Stamp Album* is nothing if not scrupulously truthful. A painstaking record of the disappearing details of everyday life (sights and sounds; habits and objects; myths and folklore) as well as of the unhistoric acts of ordinary people, it tells us what no history book can.

Sergeev's style is beautifully succinct and purposely terse. This translation — Sergeev's first appearance in English — reflects the spareness of the original and, one hopes, the clarity. But because the world *Stamp Album* documents is long gone and because it was never open to outsiders to begin with, outsiders now may find themselves at an occasional loss with respect to certain allusions. The Notes at the back should help fill in the blanks.

Joanne Turnbull

BEFORE THE WAR

I'm lying on Mama's trestle bed and through the planed partition I can see white, flour-flecked figures in my room cutting plump rolls of dough with carving knives. A small gland in my neck has become inflamed. The stately surgeon bicycles over from Malakhovka. I call him Gastronome. He always brings me chocolates and one fine afternoon under a burning light on the dining-room table — Mama and Granny are holding me down — he operates.

"A job fit for a young lady. The stitches are so neat no one will notice."

I no longer need my pacifier, but I hate to give it up. Papa leads me down an embankment, puts the pacifier on the rail, and points:

"Look, there's a train coming."

I stare into the distance towards Malakhovka. The train rushes past. When the rail reappears, it's bare. I feel better now it's over, not sad anymore; but the bareness scares me.

Everything must be washed; we wash a slender carrot from the garden in the slop-barrel. Nothing happens to Vadik. For my dysentery, Doctor Nikolaevsky prescribes a vile, salty-sweet medicine white as clotted milk. My stomach aches for years.

Anna Aleksandrovna, the nun from the Tikhonovs', brings the news:

"Some children — the flowers of our life — pushed Doctor Nikolaevsky off a train. Going full speed."

CHILDREN ARE THE FLOWERS OF OUR LIFE is written

on my favorite little fork. The big ones read: VACHA LABOR FACTORY. The iron knives and forks smell for a long time of what they've been used for. At lunch on the veranda, Mama/Granny stop me just as I'm about to cut:

"That's the herring knife!"

The spoons are nice, especially the teaspoons. They are silver, engraved with St. George's insignia and the surname SAZIKOV. We don't know anyone by that name.

Avdotia had a little boy staying with her: his name was Marxlen Angelov. Because his father is a Bulgarian revolutionary. Yurka Tikhonov didn't understand at first, and asked him again:

"Mark Twain Angelov?"

Papa knows someone at work named Vagap Basyrovich.

Papa wanted to name me Viktor; Mama named me after Andrei Bolkonsky. In the hospital, the woman in the bed next to hers sneered:

"What sort of a peasant name is that?"

Then she gave birth. She named the baby Vilor. Mama taunted:

"What sort of a churchy name is that?"

The woman was indignant: "V-I-L-O-R: Vladimir Ilyich Lenin Originator of the Revolution."

Mama's heart sank.

Mama and Granny are always afraid:

"Don't pick that up: it has germs!"

"Don't touch that cat: it may be rabid!"

"See that dog: mind it doesn't bite you!"

"See that man: mind he doesn't hit you!"

I look around, I tense up, I feel wet under my armpits and

suddenly tired. I run to Mama, to Granny, to some soothing pastime — so as to be alone and in peace.

It soothes me and amuses me to leaf through my motley books of rhymes:

> Anna Vanna, now our crew
> Wants to see a kangaroo...
>
> Hippopotamus sank to the bottom-most...
>
> You naughty little girl, you,
> Where'd you muddy your left shoe?
>
> In a shop on the Arbat
> Her teeth began to smart...
>
> He hadn't bathed, he hadn't shaved...
>
> Soviet people told the Dnieper...
>
> Never you envy your neighbor,
> Even if he's wearing specs.
>
> That's that funny man you meet
> Strolling down Basseiny Street...
>
> My acquaintance Crocodile...
>
> Maybe we may fight again...
>
> Then Grandpa needs his bromide...

I feel cozy copying portraits of little Pushkin and Marshal Voroshilov into my Pushkin Anniversary copybooks. Voroshilov is the best of all leaders, the only one better is Stalin, the nicest, kindest, most soothing — part and parcel of my childhood.

"THANK YOU COMRADE STALIN FOR OUR HAPPY CHILDHOOD," I pictured a low winter sun, four-story apartment houses with big windows — like those new schools — people strolling along broad sidewalks, and children pulling sleds. All this slightly downhill.

No one taught me to read and write, I learned all by myself. In 1938, bearing down with a red pencil on the first page of Stalin's new *Concise History of the Communist Party*, I etched an indelible SHIT. Papa didn't notice at first and nearly went off with it to his political study group. The book had to be taken to Granny's and burned in her stove. I didn't catch it. What's more, Granny cooed:

"Our very own saboteur."

The boys say they caught a spy in the house next to ours. He spent nights in the bathroom sewing military secrets under his skin above the elbow.

The grown-ups say the pictures on the covers of my Pushkin Anniversary copybooks are counterrevolutionary. Turn the picture of Kalinin on the tear-off calendar upside down and he looks like Radek. Radek's the one who makes up all the political jokes. They haven't shot him because then who would there be left to write the lead articles in *Pravda* and *Izvestia*?

In a beautiful blue history book for fifth graders, I find a patently fascist symbol on the button of Lenin's grammar-school uniform.

Barto prompts me:
"Our neighbor Ivan Petrovich
Sees everything the wrong way."

The woman activist from the Red Study Corner explains:

"They've arrested Hoffman for having a photograph of Trotsky."

A former partisan from the Far East, Hoffman kept a pair of German shepherds inside his fence. Our mothers hated him: he always cut in line waving his red pass.

R e d p a s s: the grown-ups say the words slowly, cautiously. But they aren't a bit shy about calling our house the Big House; it's the biggest house on our lane — five floors and a semi-basement. The squat houses on either side have sunk down, but our beautiful house was put up in 1914 right on the Kaplya River. When a tram trundles down our Kapelsky Lane, the windowpanes rattle in their frames.

On the corner of First Meshchanskaya Street there used to be a church called the Trinity on the Kaplya. It was built by a tavern-keeper whose drinks, by agreement with the customers, were all short a *kaplya* (a drop). Now there is nothing there but bareness and puddles pocked with bright red shards of brick — the same as in Granny's yard. Surrounding the bareness is a tall, gray building with the local post office. Coming up First Meshchanskaya there's a colonnade: Papa leads me along the elevation between the ribbed columns. Papa is enchanted by new, m o d e r n First Meshchanskaya, only the windows in the buildings are low. And running down the middle of the street there used to be *such lovely trees*: they cut them all down.

On a wintry side street a coatless man, swollen and bespectacled, asks Mama for twenty kopecks. She gives him a ruble:

"Poor soul."

When Mama and I go i n t o w n, she usually buys me a hot Mikoyan cutlet on a round roll and waits while I eat it.

Mikoyan cutlets, I think, are better than Mama's, but I can't tell her that: she'd be hurt. And I feel awkward chewing in front of the people in the bakery — as if I'm being rushed.

Ancient ladies inquire over the counter:

"Are the French buns fresh?"

Ads on the sides of buildings:

HE DESERVES JAM AND PRESERVES!

ISN'T IT TIME YOU HAD
A CAN OF TENDER TASTY CRAB!

One evening they show cartoons on a firewall in the yard: the three little pigs croon:

"Boys and girls, eat more ham!"

Every payday Papa brings home two hundred grams of bologna he's had sliced specially in the shop, paper-thin.

Mama gives the *Brockhaus and Efron Encyclopedia* to a book peddler; it took up all the shelves on one side of the marble windowsill. When Papa comes home from work he is horrified — now all we have is the *Small Soviet Encyclopedia* and it isn't even complete.

Papa doesn't cut articles out of the Encyclopedia or paste over the portraits of people who have since been arrested.

That summer in Udelnaya our half-mad lodger Varvara Mikhailovna showed Mama two booklets, one with Timiryazev on the cover, the other with Stalin:

"Look what a noble face he has. But that one has no forehead at all!"

Papa is telling us about things at work, at Timiryazev: a colleague of his, associate professor Dyman, has taken to turning up in church on Sundays and spying out acquaintances. Has to: he's a Party man.

"He's a paltry man," Mama chimes in.

The Dymans call on us several times every winter.

Bolshaya Ekaterininskaya Street. We're sitting on a little bench in front of Granny's stove. As soon as the fire catches we quick shut the door: mustn't waste wood. Gazing at the fire is hypnotic, but we're not allowed. Today, though, we are.

Granny is going through the velvet-covered family album with the gold clasps and cutting the heads off tsarist uniforms with shoulder straps:

"Save their faces at least!"

Sometimes she talks to the wall:

"Sadist!" Or to the window: "Syphilitic!"

I've heard her confess to Mama in a whisper:

"When I find his picture on a piece of newspaper in the WC, I still use it, I do, but I turn it over, it's a person's face after all..."

Granny is so much a part of me that one day I humble a boy in the yard with the boast:

"Only your mama borned you, but my mama *and* my granny borned me!"

No one tries to tell me what I can and can't say. Even so, I only once told a terrible lie in the yard: I said my papa was a tsarist general. Again I didn't catch it.

Another time when I bragged, they were even pleased. Kayanna — our neighbor Klara Ivanovna — bent down and said:

"What was that you said, Andrei? Say it again."

"My papa is a military man, my mama is a military woman, and my granny is a military old lady."

Badges of rank and their different shapes fascinate me: cubes, rectangles, four diamonds with a star, red cuffs, chevrons on sleeves. Most splendid of all are the stripes down the sides of Cossack trousers; most striking is Marshal Budyonny's handlebar moustache.

The spire on the Budyonny helmet is a military ruse: if the spire sticks up out of the trench, the enemy will shoot straight through it.

In one of my books of nursery rhymes, Budyonny visits a kindergarten and lets the children touch his saber and his moustache. The book is called *Budyonnickies*.

I'm having my hair cut at the new barbershop in the Central House of the Red Army. I can't take my eyes off the mannish woman in the flight uniform. Is that Raskova? Grizodubova? Osipenko? Mama thinks nothing of asking. That's Vera Lomako. She's also training to fly non-stop from Moscow to the Far East.

Names from my childhood:
Maksim Gorky, the airplane; *Chelyuskin*, the icebreaker
Otto Yulevich Shmidt, Captain Voronin
Molokov, Kamanin, Lyapidevsky, Levanevsky, et al
Chkalov, Baidukov, Belyakov
Gromov, Yumashev, Danilin
Raskova, Grizodubova, Osipenko

Papanin, Krenkel, Shirshov, Fyodorov
Badigin, Trofimov

The most important is Valery Chkalov. Lots of boys younger than me have been named after him. Then one day the mothers are telling each other something and crying. They say Chkalov has crashed into a scrap heap. I picture our back entrance, the Tatar yard-keeper's hut, and the wooden garbage bin — with a little plane sticking up out of it.

The Tatar yard-keeper's family may be eyeing it from their hut.

Tatar rag-and-bone men call out under the windows:
"Bring us yer things! Br-r-ring-da-ding!"
The rag-and-bone men are brought into the kitchen through the back door. Nannies frighten little children with those large sacks of theirs.

Nannies are everywhere. I once had a nanny named Matyonna — Maria Antonovna Venediktova — a friend of Granny's. She took me to different churches and may have had me quietly baptized. Mama/Granny didn't baptize me d e l i b e r a t e l y: they said that when I grew up, if I wanted to, I could do it myself.

Down quiet side streets orderly g r o u p s of five or six boys and girls stroll with elderly instructresses conversing in foreign languages.
"I've put mine in a German group."
"Mine's in a French one."
"Why did you put yours in an English one?"
I wasn't in any group. Nor did I go to the kindergarten on the other side of the fence.

In Udelnaya, glaziers come down the road shouldering wooden boxes:

"Panes fer frames! Panes fer frames!"

Or odd-job men:

"Fix it, patch it, reattach it!"

Once a summer Ivan Ivanovich turns up from the village of Vyalki. With a long-handled shovel he scoops the shit out from under the outhouse and wheels it away in a metal barrow to a pit by the gate.

In Udelnaya and in Moscow, scraggy one-legged organ grinders wander by: *t y u r l y u r l y u*. They're one-legged because of their one-legged organs.

In the yards they're selling C h i n e s e   n u t s (peanuts). I don't like them, they smell of earth and castor oil, but if you shell one and split it open you'll see — on one of the halves at the top — the little head of a bearded Chinaman.

Countrywomen go from yard to yard hawking raspberry rooster lollipops — a mother's nightmare:

"All those germs!"

On parade days First Meshchanskaya Street is full of lollipop women.

They tried renaming First Meshchanskaya (Commoner) Street First Grazhdanskaya (Citizen), then went back to First Meshchanskaya.

People are walking down First Meshchanskaya. Few of them are tall. So few, in fact, that boys would invariably call each tall one a long name — *Uncle-Grab-That-Sparrow.*

On ordinary days on First Meshchanskaya you see carts, sledges, covered wagons, horses. As many horses as cars. The horses don't interest me, the cars vary. As a rule they're gray and rickety. But every once in a while a big, black shiny one tears down the middle of the street, tootling in a treble something like:

"Ovid-ovid!"

On the corner of Third Meshchanskaya by the cooperative, by S o k o l o v ' s, there's a Mosselprom stall selling toffees, caramels, candies with white or pink fillings, and hollow chocolate eggs. They say the eggs used to have wonderful little trinkets inside. But all that's e x p e n s i v e.

Most tempting of all — because I can't have them — are the peddlers' homemade toys:

A paper ball filled with sawdust on an elastic string: to thwack the boy sitting next to you with.

A nightingale: a bright red wooden sleeve with a lead core. Twirl it while squeezing, and it erupts in raspy trills.

A bumblebee: a clay cylinder on a string or a twig. Spin it and it buzzes.

A howler: a fingerstall on a short tube with a crosspiece. Blow on it and it howls, another mother's nightmare:

"From mouth to mouth, all those germs again!"

A babbitt toy pistol with a spring on a screw. The powder plugs make a loud bang, a mother's worst nightmare:

"He'll blow his hand off!"

So as to outdo the peddlers, my parents take me to a little toy shop on First Meshchanskaya and buy me a box — like a matchbox, only bigger — of ten painted toy soldiers and a captain, nestled in cotton.

I add to my collection, one or two soldiers at a time. On a visit to Bolshaya Ekaterininskaya, I show Grandfather:

"Infantryman, cavalryman, standard-bearer, bugler, machine-gunner."

Granfather points to one running on the attack in a gas mask: "Sic'emer."

On Kapelsky Lane, while Mama is cooking in the kitchen, I play with my soldiers on the oak parquet floor. There's only one table: it doubles as Papa's desk. On the radio they're giving a lecture: *Did the garden of Gethsemane really exist?*

Every morning at ten o'clock I listen to a children's program:

> There lived in a garret
> Forty-four parrots:
> Forty-four parrots
> Is a lot to feed.
> There lived in a garret
> Nasty black bedbugs:
> The pests were told to leave —
> Or be roiled and boiled,
> Toasted and roasted,
> For the forty-four parrots as feed

I also listen to fairy tales and stories. I'm always spellbound, so long as it's not:

Read by Nikolai Litvinov: he sounds like he's wheedling, his voice is s m a r m y, as if every word were a lie.

After the children's program comes one for housewives featuring activist wives, who've won bicycles, and Khetagurova girls.

One of the songs is called *The Girls Are Off to the Far East.* Another is about a heroic switchman:

His life he may well lose
But he will never choose
To let enemies destroy the track.

Mama only turns the radio off at bedtime or when there's something on about Pavlik Morozov.

At eight o'clock, Papa listens to the news s u m m a r y.

Sometimes the Comintern station transmits *No Pasaran* from Madrid. All the broadcasts are crackly; the crackliest are the ones from Madrid and the ones that have been r e c o r d e d o n t a p e.

Papa takes me for a ride on the metro. I gasp in wonder when the train comes up over the Moscow River and the Kremlin appears out the window with its r u b y stars. Everyone knows that the most beautiful station is Kievskaya.

Over the November holidays Papa takes me to see the illuminations and shows me the new locomotives, the JOSEPH STALIN and the FELIX DZERZHINSKY, decorated with ribbons like the horses in my books.

I'm voting — just like a big person. Papa lifts me up and I drop my ballot into the urn: for Bulganin.

In our yard, I'm like everyone else, I want to be like everyone else. I'm afraid of Arkasha from the annex, but I lord it over Rafik — nicknamed Rickets — from the yard-keeper's hut. I sled down our hill standing up — not a success. Because of being clumsy, I avoid playing hopscotch on the asphalt. I play war and hide-and-seek, and once I played mother's-little-girl.

If I forget the time, Mama grabs me by the scruff of the neck:

"W e t a s a w e t r a t."

Even without her embarrassing me like that, it's not easy: I always feel annoyed (that I don't move well or fast enough) and hurt (though no one has hurt me). I become tense, tire easily, fly into uncontrollable rages. When a little girl from the fourth floor starts arguing with me, I hit her on the head with the blade of a shovel so that her head bleeds. Mama runs and apologizes, then tries to shame me. I feel not shame, but horror: what have I done, what will they do to me now?

(I don't know whether or not to believe what Mama remembered later:

"You always wanted to be a yard-keeper. You said: 'I'll get up early, take my shovel, and when people come along, I'll whisk the snow right under their feet — whisk! whisk!' ")

Scrawny, hungry Nyusha the milkmaid comes into the kitchen with the milk can. She pours out a mug of milk then pours it back to show that the can is full. If it isn't full, the milk sloshes and slops. I bring her a v i l e c o n c o c t i o n: cucumber pickles and jam. Our neighbor Ekaterina Dmitrievna sees me and says that where she comes from in the Ukraine they eat cucumbers with honey. Mama doesn't say anything. Papa praises me glumly:

"Simply marvelous, how vile!"

Once I heard Nyusha whispering to Mama that her sons the pilots had come for a visit and she was a f r a i d of them.

Granny likes to physic others, Mama is always physicking herself.

Words from my childhood: cups, mustard plasters, blue light, calcex, aspirin, quinacrine, sulfanilamide, digitalis, adonilene, salsoline, diuretin, phenobarbital, papaverine, phytin, purgene.

I like it in the apothecary. Outside everything is dirty, derelict.

But in the apothecary — the whiteness, the neatness, the orderlinesss — it's almost beautiful.

My teeth ache constantly. In Moscow, Mama takes me to Doctor Barskaya on First Meshchanskaya Street; in Udelnaya, to Doctor Salanchevskaya on Severnaya. Both women are old, not very tall, look-alikes; both pump the drill with their foot. Mama explains:

"Now a Chinese bee is going to fly into your mouth. It won't sting you."

Scarlet fever. The district doctor passes sentence: clap him in the hospital. And leaves. Mama is horrified: who knows what they'll do to him in the hospital! Granny — who works in a hospital — takes charge:

"When the ambulance comes, say they've already taken him."

In a high black taxi Granny spirits me to Bolshaya Ekaterininskaya Street.

The only time I was ever visited by a private physician, r e c o m - m e n d e d b y f r i e n d s, he told me to squat down, then listened to my knees crack:

"You're on your last legs, last legs, ought to be thrown right out."

I'm not on my last legs in Udelnaya: it's quieter there and I'm alone more.

Towards evening the heat abates and I feel like running. I race from the well to the gate then stride back shielding my eyes against the blinding sun.

Papa often takes me for walks. In Moscow he comes home too late.

Papa isn't afraid that a cat may be rabid, that a dog will bite, that a man might hit me. He passes between a horse and a cow and isn't afraid that the horse will kick me or that the cow will gore me.

Papa's jokes:

"An old woman is standing in church, praying. Suddenly she notices something white and round on the ground. She kneels down and feels around for it: 'Ugh! Forgive me, Lord. I thought it was a 20-kopeck piece, but it was only someone's spittle.'"

"A young lady is repeatedly invited to dance, but always refuses. Finally one gentleman asks: 'Why is it that you won't dance?' And she replies: 'Whayne ah daynce, thayne ah swayte, aynd whayne ah swayte, thayne ah stink.' "

I ask Papa to tell me something interesting, something about spies. Papa doesn't know anything about them. Instead he tells me about the real-life jewel thief Sonka-Golden-Hand and the fictional detective Nat Pinkerton. Across the river, in Chudakovo, he shows me a shabby manor house:

"I used to have a small bulldog revolver. I was expecting a search at home so I left the gun on a beam between some logs and paneling: it fell into the breach, from the second floor. It's probably still there."

I pick a small, crude quasi-crowbar up off the ground.

"A jimmy," says Papa and explains what it is, what it's for and for whom.

"One bitter winter highwaymen ambushed a sleigh. The coachman pointed a smoked sausage at them and bellowed: 'I'll kill you!' The highwaymen fled. Toot-tootle-toot: some sausages shoot. Before the Bolsheviks, a horse-drawn tram went from the station in Udelnaya to Chudakovo. There were some grand dachas. Old woman Klepikova was killed by bandits one winter when she stayed on alone. She wouldn't open the door. They burned the house down."

Mama wakes before dawn: the window creaked, someone was trying to break in. Thieves press rags soaked in chloroform to sleepers' faces.

Granny brings us a whistle j u s t i n c a s e: the neighbors will hear it and come running.

It's not safe to walk home from the station late at night. Chances are you'll be stripped in the alder bushes before Novaya Malakhovka, just beyond the new foot-bridge where those t w o Chinamen drowned.

Two Chinamen drowned is from my walks with Papa. They were students at the Communist University of Eastern Workers and went in wading, drunk.

Sukhovolsky, an acquaintance of Papa's (he's older than Papa), remembers the Chinamen, too, and chuckles: in the very shallowest place. He wears a blouse belted with a Caucasian sash, riding breeches, and slippers. He invites us to his dacha in Bykovo:

"I have a harmonium! I'll play you Bortnyansky! Such music: the walls weep!"

From Sukhovolsky:

"Lacrimosa!"

There's only one policeman in Udelnaya and he's at the station.

Sometimes he struts down International Street, stumpy and barrel-chested in his new diagonal uniform. Mothers stare after him:

"NKVD."

They recall:

"An Army commander — Vacietis — used to live at the old Goat woman's. He did gymnastics every morning and doused himself with cold water."

Volodka, the younger brother of our lodger Sasha, takes Shulgin's *Days* away from Mama:

"You could be arrested for that book."

"Take it," says Mama, and when he's gone: "Dirty rascal!"

One Sunday Volodka, in the company of other lodgers from other dachas, asserts that the word *kerosene* comes from the firm *Kero and Son* — the first outfit ever to sell the stuff. All great men are Jewish: Columbus, Cromwell, Napoleon, Karl Marx. Hitler's Jewish too.

After lunch dacha owners and their lodgers gather on verandas around the gramophone. People spend years preparing, saving, and debating before buying themselves opera glasses, or a thermos, or a gramophone.

Everyone owns essentially the same records.

Out of ideology: *Higher and Higher, Bike Tour March, Divers' March, A Komsomol Member is Piloting the Plane.*

Out of learnedness: Chaliapin.

Out of love: some own Lemeshev, others Kozlovsky. Lemeshev lovers are waging a desperate and hopeless war against Kozlovsky.

For one's own pleasure: Kozin or gypsy songs.

For parties: Utyosov and foreign tangos, foxtrots, rumbas. The records are not foreign, every last one was made in either the Noginsk or the Aprelevka factory.

Parties mean dancing. Papa doesn't dance. Mama knows how to waltz. I'm told that Varlamov's *Sweet Sue* is Chinese music. I go

off into a corner of the veranda and f o x t l o t Chinese-style —
with both index fingers raised.

Gramophone music was nothing like radio music. On the radio
there were operas, Pyatnitsky's folk choir, songs by Soviet
composers, variations on songs by Soviet composers, songs about
Stalin.

Radio music was far less appealing than gramophone music.

Yet over the years of the radio's always being on, I picked up,
came to love, and memorized what was missing in life itself — the
vivid and the exotic:

> Glinka's sextet
> The Bullfighter's aria from *Carmen*
> The Bullfighter and the Andalusian
> La Cucaracha
> Tiritomba
> Madrid, ay-ay-a

I like to sing along: they say I have a good ear. Granny, Mama
and Papa want me to take music lessons.

That means piano. But the music school isn't accepting piano
students, the Jews there take violin: if anything happens, they can
just tuck the violin under their arm and run.

Crazy Aunt Vera never played her VOIGT upright. Granny,
Mama and Papa refused to take it, most likely out of scrupulousness.
In early '39 Granny found a good, inexpensive OFFENBACHER,
which Papa bought. Inexpensive: five thousand rubles! It's clear
where such a large sum came from: Papa had just been paid for his
book. What's not clear is how that high, large i n s t r u m e n t
wedged into our 13 square meters.

I poke the keys. I think of every key as a letter; if I know the
words, then I can pick out any song I like on the keys.

The one music teacher Granny had known for years, a Czech named Aleksandr Aleksandrovich Shvarts, was very old. Another music teacher, a woman, brought me Gedike, made me tap a sounding board with a pencil, put several volumes of the *Small Soviet Encyclopedia* under me, and droned on about letter-keys. Enraged, I sassed her to her back:

"Toodle-oo, Meany-malou!"

I caught it.

On the tram, Mama falls into conversation with a serious little girl of about eight carrying her sheet music in a folder with a picture of a lyre.

"I'm taking lessons from Lyubov Nikolaevna Basova, she's the very best."

Gifted children study with Lyubov Nikolaevna in Gorchakov's house on Pushkin Square:

"After that sforzando, Milchik intuitively pedaled..."

I am not gifted. You cannot drive me to the piano, nor can you bribe me. I go to music lessons unprepared, like someone without their clothes on. I shift in my seat.

Listening to the gramophone or the radio was easier. Even the latest news was more interesting than drills on the piano. I open the newspaper. Grandfather reads *Izvestia*, I read *Pravda*, like Papa. I already know what they write about what. I'm getting used to it. Then one day I see a stern Hitler on the front page and our Molotov in the background. The woman activist from the Red Study Corner comes out into the yard:

"No more using the word 'fascist' as a term of abuse."

A time of amazement sets in.

Papa's young colleague, whom I call Uncle Volodya (about

the only person my parents are happy to invite home), tells us that in Western Byelorussia and Lithuania they were not glad to see the Red Army:

"They stood and wept."

He has brought me a 30-kopeck/2-zloty coin from 1835 and a 20-cent piece with a galloping knight on it.

Estonian crowns with their castle look like gold coins.

The shops are full of Latvian candies: *Laima chocolates*. Klara Ivanova translates the name. A little rusty, she at first reads *Laima* as *Saima* (household).

"Laima, let me see, that's 'happiness'."

Latvian candies are a hundred times better than our *Red October*, and the wrappers are so beautiful — we don't have anything like them. And you should see their cigarette boxes!

The grown-ups demur:

"Where do they get the tobacco? Probably pack them with peat."

On the last day of the war with Finland, after the armistice, Papa's brother Fyodor is killed near Vyborg.

Those who return are amazed at the spitefulness of the Finns:

"A Finnish sniper sitting in a tree shoots till he's out of cartridges."

"A nurse bends over a wounded Finn: he knifes her!"

On the radio and in the papers they never refer to the Finnish Army or Finnish soldiers. Only to bands and bandits or, at best, to Shützcorps men.

Ogonyok's first issue for the year 1940 says that the Red Army, at the request of Finland's worker-peasant government, is helping the working people to drive out landowners and capitalists.

Our Udelnaya lodger Sasha returns from Riga amazed at the spitefulness of the Latvians:

"They hate us! Getting a shave at the barber's, I was afraid he'd cut my throat!"

Sasha brought a lot of unusual things back from Latvia: striped underpants with an ivory clasp for Lyonka; bright dresses and blouses for his wife Dusya and Volodya's Nadya; a whistling tea kettle; a nickel-plated German cigarette lighter with a shepherd on it; and a pencil sharpener in the shape of a fine little automobile.

The little automobile soon joins my enviable things. In a silk-lined brass box from a bottle of *Bilitis* perfume (Ralle, Moscow), I have a Tsar's Tea tin decorated with Chinese women; a steel American etui for ten Gillette razor blades; a mother-of-pearl purse; a polished marble lamina; a silver puzzle ring with a ruby; Granny's favorite charm — a green frog with a forget-me-not; a tiny jug from the Caucasus decorated in enamel — also a charm; a copper token for refugees; and a little icon of Saint Ksenia missing one lug.

Grandfather's presents: an ancient one-kopeck coin known as a "fish scale"; a ten-kopeck piece from Peter's reign; a 5-kopeck piece with an eagle in the clouds from Elizabeth's reign; ten-kopeck pieces with holes through them from Catherine's reign.

Rare things all: no one else has them. I want, want to have, what no one else has. I want what is beautiful: one comes across it so rarely...

The mannequin's head in the hairdresser's window strikes me as the height of French-court elegance: its features are fine and light, unlike the features of the women one sees in the street.

Bloody, bright-scarlet spittle on the snow is beautiful. So are the sky blue lion and the unicorn on our toilet bowl. Medals and badges are beautiful. The tsars in my book and on my stamps are beautiful. The last tsar was N i c h o l a s t h e T h i r d.

My stamps are in a large — the size of a ledger — unlined, plain green copybook. Mama pasted them in in order: England with Victorias and Georges on the first page; France with Libertes on the second; then Italy; then Germany with Lessings and Leibnizes, and so on, from West to East.

At first Mama glued a corner of each stamp with seccotine, but the stamps soon became saturated and the corners turned dark. Then she looked to see how Yurka Tikhonov did it and began mounting the stamps on little s q u a r e s. It is extraordinary how even the plainest stamps, if you look at them long enough, are still beautiful.

Lyonka, our lodger Sasha's son, does not like beautiful things. He can't even tell the difference between what's beautiful and what isn't. Actually, he's nothing like me.

Every summer, with Papa's help, I fence off a corner of our yard with some old boards to make a house with a door that has small straps for hinges and a latch. The roof is covered with tarpaper scraps, the table by the window I made myself.

Mama and Sasha's Dusya once sat Lyonka and me down at my table to eat lunch. His smacking lips and grease-smeared face so disgusted me that I hit him and ran away. He offended my sensibilities.

The next day I fed him rabbit wood sorrel and "goat nuts". I pretended to eat them too, but he was greedy and grabbed them right out of my mouth. When his stomach began to ache, he told. Sasha didn't dare hit me, but he complained to Mama:

"You are such a lovely person, Evgenia Ivanovna. How is it your son is a sadist?"

My conscience didn't bother me, on the contrary:

> Little Lyonka Shiteater
> Goes trot-trot into town,
> While from out of his ass,
> Goat nuts come raining down!

Lyonka's grandfather's name is Leon Abramovich, his grandmother's is Maria Efimovna. Mama has her doubts:

"Can't be Maria! Must be Matlya."

Matlya reads to Lyonka in a singsong voice:

> Syoma's ben goane all summer loang,
> Ben away in the Arktek ben Syoma...

She's never heard of the Artek summer camp, but they talk about the Arctic on the radio all the time. She plucks a rooster and croons wistfully:

> Bound fer Odessa, wound up in Kherson
> Coaght in 'n ambush one 'n' oall,
> An outpost here, Makhno's men there,
> 'N' only ten grenades left in oall.

Before that Yura and Borya — both slightly older than me — lived with us. Borya was a boy after my own heart: I called him my "heart case", an expression I'd picked up from Granny/Mama. Under Borya's influence I became entranced — as never before or since — by nature. We spent whole days in Little Pines — a special place at the end of our yard above a stream where the earth had never been turned up and nothing had ever been planted, where only grass and pines grew. We ate sorrel, corn flags, and wild mustard. In Little Pines or by the bathing place, we netted mourning cloaks, swallowtails, huge dragonflies, and fine coral and turquoise damselflies, we kicked brown frogs and picked up green ones.

The frogs jumped into the water. Horsetails you could pull apart — joint by joint — stood above the water. Water plants grew magically and minnows shimmered under the water. Water lilies lay heavily on the water. While water striders whisked over the water in their own round wakes, as if on skates. Snags stuck up out of the water. It never occurred to me that all this, too, was beautiful.

There is no greater happiness than squelching barefoot along the warm, squashy marsh bottom and sinking into it ankle-deep, while peering all around. A child's paradise lies by the stream.

We bathed not along the bank, but in an enclosed bathing place, which Papa and Uncle Ivan built every year. As long as a grown-up was watching, I was allowed to climb carefully down the little ladder and take a dip. The water was too warm to be refreshing.

Mama's cousin, Uncle Igor, a military cadet, once flipped backwards off the ladder, flashed a gum, and sent bubbles up from under the water.

He asked me a riddle: "How do you spell chocolate? Is it ChAcolate or chUcolate?" I was too ashamed to try and answer.

It was from Igor I learned Ryzan Artillery College songs:

> For the defense of freedom and peace
> We have grenades and shrapnel ready...
> Over field and stream
> Our detachment marched.

> Hail, Byelorussian brother
> Forever dear.
> Woe to the Polish gentry...

Borya and I had grand times that one summer. Otherwise my best friend and comfort was the Tikhonovs' stuttering lodger Vadik. He was s l o w . We would weewee over the fence, then scramble up into the tall apple trees and sing away:

> Fishing a river for fishes
> An old man lost his britches...

> The man from Havana ate a banana...

> An aeroplane flits,
> Its motor hums,
> A Komsomol man sits,
> Stuffing plums

It was easy to tease:

> And in it Lyonka sits
> Stuffing plums

Our favorite things were all indecent. A song:

> A small chicken broiled, a small chicken boiled
> Went strolling down the street to the station.
> Soon he was stopped, soon he was foiled:
> They asked for identification.
> He burst into tears, pooed in his pants,
> Then begged for some paper, Alas!
> Don't have any? Then newsprint will do,"
> And he began wiping his ass.

Every winter Mama, Papa, and I went to Usachev Street to visit Varvara Mikhailovna. She had an album full of indecent German postcards, three to a page:

two little boys sitting on chamber pots;

a little boy and a little girl sitting on chamber pots;

a squire and a young lady sitting on chamber pots back to back;

a squire and a young lady sitting on chamber pots facing each other;

a squire and a young lady on chamber pots in just their undergarments;

a squire and a young lady on chamber pots in their overcoats;

a lady and a moustachioed gentleman on chamber pots;

a grandfather and a grandmother on chamber pots.

Papa said that these postcards were pornographic.

Vadik and I go off by ourselves to the shed, pull down our pants and show each other our behinds. This is called frucking. Vadik says that where he lives in Sokolniki, boys fruck with girls.

Everyone has a different word for it:

>Mama and Papa: tinkling
>
>Granny: trinkling
>
>Vadik: weeweeing
>
>Borya and Yura: doing number one
>
>Andrei Zvavich: peeing
>
>Uncle Igor: sprinkling
>
>Yurka Tikhonov: pissing

There are other series, too: bottom, rumpet, rear, Madame Derriere, ass.

Mama has accepted the fact that we s w e a r. Shit and ass are almost all right. Fruck is not allowed. We keep quiet about frucking. And keep an ear out for new swear words. We gleefully listen in on a neighbor telling Papa about hunting:

"And there we were just farting along."

Yurka Tikhonov — he's four years older than us — came home with a good word — only he forgot it:

"Something like 'can't'."

Yurka calls sparrows "Yids", and those pretty wagtails "hagtails".

When it rains, he says: "God's pissing"; when it thunders: "God's farting."

He threatens:

> I'll tear off yer legs 'n' give ya pegs,
> 'N' make ya walk from here ta the dregs!

He likes to stuff white dandelion puffs into wide-open mouths. If you say *What?*, he says: Shit on a nut, wipe your butt.

Yurka shat all over the place and, to our amazement, pulled up his pants without wiping himself.

In a good mood, Yurka would tell us about the cinema:

"A field. Then right in the middle of it an explosion! People running..."

"An old man sitting by a stream fishing... But see, he's a spy."

Also from the cinema:

> Sailors stroll on deck
> Smoking cigarettes
> While poor Charlie Chaplin
> Picks up all the ends.

> The thunder clapped, the clouds crapped,
> And the air smelled like shit...

A joke Yurka made up: "A barin builds a village and decides to name it after the first thing he sees in his path. He walks out onto the road and sees a pair of britches lying right there. So he names his village Britches. The next day, a peasant from another village is going to market. The barin's peasant asks: 'What're you selling?' 'Nuts.' 'You call those nuts? In our barin's Britches, *these* are nuts!'"

Yurka's mother, Natalia Sergeevna, nags Yurka about his g u t t e r   t a l k. He quacks:
"Aw, shut up!"

With Yurka I can shoot with a bow. His semi-basement is full of old furniture made of m a h o g a n y. Mahogany makes the straightest, most accurate arrows.

With Yurka I can play aeroplane.
"Do we have contact?"
"Yes, we have contact!"
Long games make him impatient.

We played soldiers more seriously than the grown-ups played chess. Uncle Igor taught us: on the croquet pitch in front of the veranda we made a Mannerheim line. Barbed-wire entanglements, trenches, pillboxes, cannons. Granny brought us a s p a r k l i n g   m a c h i n e - g u n — turn the handle and sparks fly from the flint in the muzzle. Soldiers fall. Igor rubs the wire with wax and burns it through with a match. A tank rolls out into the breach. A wooden battleship sails along the path. The war goes on and on. Neither I nor Vadik wins — we'll pick the game up again tomorrow.

I already have a hundred toy soldiers. I know them all by face.
Using a dinner knife, a hammer, and a chisel — I get a blister

on my right hand — I construct an aeroplane and two cannons that shoot little stones, like slingshots.

And even so I'm green with envy.

Never before or since have I envied anyone so much as I envied the fat son of that man in the foreign service, Zvavich. He was also named Andrei. They lived at the old Goat woman's.

Andrei's toy soldiers were from abroad: English guardsmen in huge black hats and French infantrymen in red trousers. They could raise their arms and place a rifle on their shoulder. Compared to my crude soldiers, Andrei's were unbearably beautiful. I borrowed Aunt Vera's oils and tried painting mine — with repulsive results. I was so upset the Zvaviches felt compelled to give me one of Andrei's Frenchmen.

Soon I was wild about France — about the Napoleons from the second-hand shop, about the Paris Commune in my children's book, about the revolutions in the *Small Soviet Encyclopedia*. Neighbors of ours on Kapelsky Lane gave me a color postcard from 1912: *Cossacks seize Napoleon's baggage train*.

Two happy memories are connected with France.

The New Year's party at the Trubnikovs' inexplicably roomy and separate (like a dacha) apartment where beautiful things abounded and Granny was one of the family.

Trubnikov's son-in-law, a chemistry professor by the name of Balandin, performed magic tricks: he combined two glasses of plain water to make multi-colored waters; he set fire to a sheet of white paper, scorching the edges so that animal shapes appeared; he put on a firework display in the big room.

I forgot everything in the world — for possibly the first time. I danced by the tree with children I'd never met before as if I'd always known them. I gabbled, laughed and made friends with a little girl, meaning I pulled her down on the sofa and began twisting her legs. The grown-ups separated us, merrily, their laughter benign.

As I was leaving, the Trubnikovs presented me with a regal gift: an enormous *Images Militaires*, an album of soldiers in red trousers fighting historic battles and just plain.

Those kind Trubnikovs, if only they knew how much they did for me!

The New Year's party at their house was the one time Granny/ Mama were not afraid to take me out to call on people.

My second memory is the third of June 1939. I'm playing with my soldiers on the floor, on the veranda of our dacha. I've just turned six. Everyone is glad to see me, everyone has brought presents. Crazy Aunt Vera comes out from Moscow, gives me an i m p o r t e d French book, and flees, back to the station, so as not to meet anyone. The book is full of red and striped — tricolor — trousers. Goethe lost in thought on horseback. General Kellermann raising his cocked hat aloft on his sword...

A warm, smooth, languid day. Gathered around the table are Mama, Papa, Granny, Igor's mother Great Aunt Asya, her husband Dmitry Petrovich, and our lodgers. Everyone is smiling at me and at each other. Greater benevolence, greater happiness in childhood I never knew.

My very best birthday...

THE WAR

A small Montpensier fruit-drop tin. Beneath disfigured border guards on the box's lower edge, a tantalizing ellipsis reads: WE'LL KEEP AND PRIZE... WE'LL WATCH OUR... Only later does it occur to me that this — beginning to the left and ending to the right — is the dull, clumsy rhyme:

WHAT OCTOBER GAVE US, WE'LL KEEP AND PRIZE:
WE'LL WATCH OUR BORDERS WITH EAGLE EYES.

Enemies lurk on every border:

WHITE GUARD FINLAND: we fought the Finns.

FASCIST LATVIA, ESTONIA, LITHUANIA: it's hard to say whether we fought them or not.

LANDOWNING POLAND: we defeated it.

NAZI GERMANY: My grade-school reader has stories by Yefim Zozulya about a future war.

Advancing Red Army soldiers capture a Polish tank. The tank contains a chapel and a chemical laboratory. The Catholic Polish priest driving the tank had instructions to poison the entire vicinity. Peasants arrive, see the tank, and thank the Red Army.

German fascists take a wounded Red Army soldier prisoner and bring him to Berlin. Berlin's workers rise straight up and overthrow the fascists.

But you don't need Yefim Zozulya to tell you that Nazi Germany and fascist Italy have attacked good, republican Spain.

Murzilka, the children's magazine, is running a series about the adventures of a little Spanish boy:

Verses:

> I shot down a plane, Charita, see,
> And set fire to a black *Caproni*.

Spanish children are being brought to the USSR. No one has seen them, but everyone loves them. They know:

> The words we all know —
> Camarados, Lenin, Stalin,
> Komsomol, Madrid, Moscow.

Like other boys my age I have a Spanish costume: a plain pocket-shaped hat with a tassel in front. In Boris Yefimov's cartoon, the fascists have two tassels: one in front and one in back.

BOYAR RUMANIA didn't fight us: it didn't have the nerve.

TURKEY and PERSIA are being incited against us by IMPERIALISTIC ENGLAND and MILITARISTIC FRANCE.

Our most illustrious border is the Far East. Khetagurova girls go off to the Far East. There are those three tank drivers in the Far East. The Far East is where Karatsupa the border guard and his dog Hindu caught a hundred violators.

In one of my children's books there's a story about a spy who crosses the border using a Young Pioneer as a shield: the border guards can't shoot. As soon as the spy is across the border, he shoots the Young Pioneer in the heart. Gaidar writes the most and the best of all about boys and spies, he's t a l e n t e d.

Verses:

> In the cold gloom, the dead of night
> An enemy crossed the border
> A messenger sent by the Whites

A spy and a saboteur...
The chemical plant, the wires,
All went up in flames...

The grown-ups say Mikhalkov's verses are p o e t i c:

Alive and well
Is border guard Ninel.

FASCIST JAPAN has attacked good CHINA. In *Murzilka*, the bogatyr Ezhov is shown standing next to the legendary Zhu De. Yang, the People's son, is throwing a grenade at the Japanese. Right in front of the Japanese, a Chinese motorcyclist sails through the air and over an abyss.

The Japanese try to attack us at Lake Hasan. The Special Far Eastern Army destroys them.

The Japanese seize a Soviet steamship with Young Pioneer Misha Korolkov aboard. Where's Stalin? Misha won't tell. The Japanese major — the Japanese are always majors — fumes:

Tell us what we want to know
And you'll find sweets aplenty
In that little drawer below
Chocolates and fruit jelly.
For silly answers like these,
As many lashes as you please.

The Motherland saves Misha Korolkov.

On the Halhin-Gol River, the Japanese attack the Mongolian People's Republic. This is our one friendly border. We've been receiving good foreign things from the MPR for some time, the way we did from Riga in 1940. In conversation, the MPR is just as important as England or Poland. We're knocking the Japanese out of the MPR. Someone Papa knows was almost taken prisoner near the Halhin-Gol: his car broke down in the middle of the steppe.

Papa and Mama take me to the cinema for the first time. To the Arts cinema on Arbat Square. To see the new talkie *If There's War Tomorrow.* Our neighbor Boris Fyodorovich recommended it, those were his exact words:

"I recommend it."

Through poison gas, infantrymen advance in gas masks, cavalrymen gallop and heavy tanks crawl. One of our pilots perishes in an unequal battle. The final frames are in color. Victory. Stalin and Voroshilov on top of Lenin's Mausoleum. The song:

> We don't want war, but we will fight back,
> We'll always drive the enemy out,
> On his turf, too, we'll smash and sack,
> And put our foe to a ruthless rout.

We are strengthening our national defenses. Everyone has signed up to contribute to the OSOAVIAKHIM defense fund. A dirigible with a huge portrait of Karl Marx is in the sky. Proud *medal recipients* — Voroshilov, Hero pilots, Gaidar, Mikhalkov — are in the papers. Proud wearers of badges — Voroshilov marksmen — are in the streets. The wearers of these less prestigious badges, m e d a l m o n g e r s, sport one, two or three of them, all triangular (Ready for Labor and Defense, Ready for Sanitary Defense, Air Chemical Defense), on their jackets and short-sleeved shirts. Huge Air Chemical Defense signs are being put up on buildings. They've cut down all the trees on First Meshchanskaya Street and along the Garden Ring: the greenery gets in the way of the degassing.

The apothecaries are selling gas masks like hot-water bottles. The one place there are no gas masks and no Air Chemical Defense pamphlets is at Granny's on Bolshaya Ekaterininskaya Street. At home on Kapelsky Lane, I pull on a new gray mask with elastic ear bands and a long corrugated hose. I morbidly devour anti-gas pamphlets. Mustard gas smells of mustard, lewisite of I'm not sure what, and hydrocyanic acid of almonds. When there's a gas alert, they bang on a gong or a rail.

When the woman activist in our yard forbade us to use 'fascist' as a term of abuse, the great war was already on. From Kapelsky we watched the war as if from the dress circle: it was interesting, but no more so than the cinema, and it didn't concern us. Everyone in our communal kitchen laughed when Beck and Rydz-Smigly escaped to Rumania. Everyone chuckled when they read about the first English prisoner. He fell asleep on the front line, awoke and was amazed. The Germans, too, were amazed: they hadn't yet seen any English. The article was called: *Where Are You, Brave Tommies?*

There are pictures in *Ogonyok* of the destruction in London; of French refugees fleeing; of a German soldier in Paris by the Arc de Triomphe.

A cartoon by Boris Yefimov shows French, English and American capitalists catching money with their top hats: *Gold, gold is falling from the sky.*

My pocket atlas says the light-brown area to the west of the USSR is the Region of Germany's National Interests.

My new stamp album has a page for every country. A page for Uruguay and a page for Paraguay, though the stamps from there are negligible. There is no page for Austria or Poland or

Lithuania or Latvia or Estonia, though there are lots of stamps. Instead of Czechoslovakia, there is simply Slovakia.

Thanks to our friendship with Germany, the shops are selling Memel chicory in scarlet paper cylinders.

The byword in our yard:

"Come in! Come in! This is Berlin!"

The papers repeatedly confirmed our friendship. At noon on June 22 Molotov announced how it ended. In Udelnaya, Papa, Mama, neighbors and lodgers ran out into the lane so they could hear the radio blaring from the Bogoslovskys'.

Everyone was stunned. No one said anything memorable. Only Vadik:

"I'm going to the front — let'm kill me the way they killed Gavroche."

My parents took the Soviet Information Bureau's daily bulletins as a matter of fact: Soviet forces have abandoned this city, that town, another city. They were somewhat taken aback at the mention of Kishinev: Papa had been invited there to work and might easily have accepted — instead of our 13 square meters, we would have had a whole apartment. And they were somewhat encouraged by the fact that so far there had been no reports about Minsk and Smolensk.

That summer — not the usual time — they awarded the Stalin Prize to the inventor Kostikov. For a secret weapon, people whispered.

Conversations in the summer of '41 were short:

"Given the development of transportation today we needn't fear famine."

"Stock up on salt, groats and matches while the cooperative still has any."

"I don't know where to evacuate to — the Ukraine, Tashkent, or Kislovodsk."

"In Bykovo, an old man with a goat turned out to be a spy."

"Four women pilots bailed out of a German reconnaissance plane when it was hit and landed in the Vyalki Cemetery."

"Levanevsky didn't die at the North Pole, he flew over it to the Germans and now he's bombing Moscow."

"This all comes from the OWS — One Woman Said — wire service."

"You never know..."

On instructions from the Village Soviet, moonlighters dug a slit trench in Little Pines in exchange for a bottle of vodka.

At night a siren wailed horribly. More horrible than the siren was Levitan's sepulchral voice coming over the Bogoslovskys' radio:

"CI-ti-zens, air-RAID a-LERT!"

Mama lugged me half-asleep to the other end of our property.

Dusya clutched little Lyuska under one arm and dragged Lyonka with the other: he kept stumbling and falling to his knees.

The slit trench smelled of fresh earth, but soon turned stuffy. Lyonka smacked his lips loudly in his sleep; when the anti-aircraft banged loudly, he woke up hiccupping in fright.

The next morning the whole dacha trooped to Malakhovka to gloat: a stray bomb had crushed the little station house and one person to death. We looked for shards — there were only shards of glass.

That afternoon I combed *Pravda* for accounts of atrocities:

"Right breast severed; left breast charred; heart gouged out; sexual organ mashed."

In a piece on the bombing of Moscow, Aleksei Tolstoy wrote, as I now recall and it can't be right:

"A wounded woman was masturbating ecstatically."

I didn't know what a *sexual organ* or *masturbating* was, but the words stuck in my mind.

Towards evening from the hammock through the firs, I heard the slow steps of an older person coming down the lane. An officer threw his head back and sang an old romance in a high, wistful voice, almost to himself:

"When I was a postilion for the penny post..."

In the evening, by the Makedonka River, the Tikhonovs' lodger said to Mama:

"Andrei's lucky: he already understands everything, but they won't put him in the Army. Later he'll look back..."

Yurka Tikhonov comes to say goodbye: he's going to Tyumen, to his uncle's. I:

"To hide out in the rear?"

Yurka comes at me with his fists. Mama scolds me. How can I explain that it's just a line from *Julio Jurenito.* I didn't mean to offend anyone.

That same day, when Mama and I went back to Kapelsky Lane, the woman activist turned up: she was making a list of children to be evacuated. Mama told me to crawl under the table, then said:

"They've already taken him."

Papa's in the shed digging a shelter — so we won't have to go to Little Pines, so we'll have a place that is closer, safer — with a ceiling three beams' thick piled with earth almost to the roof. Camouflaged by the shed, it might even survive a direct hit. And if they come and evict us, we could hide there. Fortunately, we never had to.

Overlooking the Makedonka, to the right of the dump, an

alder tree stood tall as a pine. In broad daylight and single-handed, Papa sawed it deftly down before my eyes, sawed it up into logs, split the logs in our yard, and stacked them in the shed: wood for the winter. Fortunately, we barely needed it.

Frantic neighbors come running to fetch Mama:

"Evgenia Ivanovna, you can do it..."

Pavlik Khlebnikov, all grown up, had tied himself with a belt to the crown of the tallest pine overlooking the Bogoslovskys' dacha. He was flailing his arms and legs, as if he were in the water.

"Pavlik what're you doin' up there? Come down this minute!"

"All right, all right. I just wanted to see what it feels like to be a parachute jumper..."

I like to loll on the shed roof. The autumn sun is more noticeable on the black tar paper.

Overhead a plane with red stars flies leisurely. It drones not the way our planes drone — continuously — but the way German planes do — oo-oo-oo-oo-oo. Over by the Bykovo aerodrome six dull explosions resound. The plane flies back at the same easy pace. Fifteen minutes later, snub-nosed fighters are darting about the sky shooting tracer bullets.

Sometimes Lyonka climbs up after me: he's afraid of the wooden ladder with its rotten rungs. I say:

"If the Germans come, don't tell them your last name is Shafran, say it's Akimov. You're here with your mother, after all."

(Mama told the story, not to me:

"Dusya was almost five months along when she decided to get rid of it. Drank somethin' vile — did her no good at all. So I helped her. Dusya's a strappin' girl, she can take anythin'. We buried the baby in Little Pines.")

Shafran turned up unexpectedly from the hospital to fetch Lyonka, Lyuska and Dusya. He was so shaken, he kept saying the same thing over and over:

"A German pilot shot me. I saw him. He was flying so low. The doctor said he missed killing me by hair, just a hair..."

Old man Bogoslovsky returned from a volunteer corps near Smolensk:

"We lugged artillery through the mud in our arms — artillery from 1914!"

I had amassed a number of trophies: a bomb stabilizer; red (Soviet) and yellow (German) cartridge cases; pointed (Soviet) bullets and snubbed (German) bullets; and shards.

The shards were Soviet, from anti-aircraft shells. The rumbling woke me up at night and I heard mice pattering in the back of my sofa. A silent shard came to rest on the windowsill by my head. Under the Bogoslovskys' pine trees, where Borya and I used to pick lilies of the valley, shards lay on top of the pine needles, rather than buried in the ground.

I started: I could feel I wasn't alone at the Bogoslovskys'. I hid behind a pine and so did he. He could be tough and I could be proprietary, but neither one of us had any business being there.

We laid out our finds for each other. He had a few more shards than I did. Like me, he cared about stamps/coins.

Shurka Morozov lived on Krivokolennaya Street, opposite the Tikhonovs. His father worked all day in a factory in Lyubertsy, his mother was an activist. His hateful grandmother stayed home. His grandfather had been a chief of police. His last name was Garnish, supposedly Czech, probably German — he made Shurka graze the goat all day.

I would run out to meet him beyond Little Pines, by the dump.

In the summer of '41 the dump was dappled with beautiful shit-smeared tsarist bonds. Should we take them or not? We couldn't decide.

Shurka drove the goat, swore, and sang:

> There was a mean, old priest,
>> Heil Hitler!
> With an ass-backwards beast,
>> Heil Hitler!
> A she-goat for shunting shit,
>> Heil Hitler!
> Ass-backwards out of a pit.
>> Heil Hitler!

A boy with a goat (though his name's Garnish, supposedly Czech, probably German) is still not an old man with a goat; he sings *Heil Hitler*, but he's no spy.

We pour sulfur from matches into the hollow shank of a key, plug it with a nail, attach it to a string, and swing it against a log. We take cartridges apart for the powder and cook up explosions. From a piece of nickel-plated pipe — for small-bores — we cook up what's known as a w h a c k - o f f. Grown-ups shudder at the word, even before they realize it's *He'll-blow-his-hand-off!* material.

I found a round — like a sausage round — piece from an anti-aircraft shell, inserted a nail in the opening and banged it: it began heating up in my hands. I had just time enough to fling it into the stream.

We run to the Village Soviet to see the newsreel *Victory Will Be Ours*. The audience is all boys. In the newsreel, the fascists are fat, stupid, and wearing armbands. A Soviet good soldier Svejk makes easy sport of them. A former landowner parachutes down into our rear. He enters the hut of an old peasant woman: she lives in a village that once belonged to his family. The old woman quietly sends her granddaughter to inform.

It seems we understand that real Germans aren't like the ones in the newsreels. Our imaginations are fired by the sublime words:

motorized infantry, *Messerschmitt*, *Junkers-88*, *Focke-Wulf*, sturmbanfuhrer, *Dead Head* division.

People tell jokes about our Soviet soldiers. But I never heard any jokes about German ones.

The summer drags on so long that before I start school a large corn cob has grown up from a seedling in my tiny kitchen garden.

Our principal, Boris Ivanovich, who's minus a finger, looks me over and calls to someone out the window:

"Don't whistle, you're not in the forest!"

The Udelnaya school is ensconced in a vast, pre-revolutionary dacha with outbuildings and annexes. Behind them — rough-and-ready, jerry built, ancestral — are M and W. A permanent stench permeates the air at thirty paces; piles glimmer outside and in; between M and W someone has drilled a hole in the wall.

The girls squat down and weewee by the fence. You can see everything. Until then, I had thought that Shafran's little Lyuska just hadn't grown one yet.

Mama was disappointed that my teacher wasn't old and e x p e r i e n c e d, but young. Even so, she presented the young teacher with a brand new pair of galoshes.

The very first day of school, the vice-principal, Toucan, walked in in the middle of a lesson:

"Air-raid drill!"

Everyone filed outside and into the long slit trench that snaked through the yard. I wound up by the way out.

"That's even better," Mama decided. "If anythin' happens, you can just scat."

She was obsessed with the idea of flight:

"Learn to ride a bicycle. Then if you see a bicycle anywhere, you can just take it an' ride off..."

"Learn to drive a car. Then if you see a car, you can just take it and..."

Personally, she was scared to death of bicycles and cars. Besides, there was no talk in our family of leaving or fleeing or evacuating: whatever happens happens.

My homework took me no time at all. Still, seeing me bent over a copybook, Mama couldn't help singing the unforgettable:

> Been sittin' over these books so long,
> Still don't understand a word they say.
> And now the seat of my pants is gone
> So how can I go out and play?

I spent my cheerless leisure loafing about in the snow or reading.

The last children's books to come out before the war don't square with what I see around me. *The Wonderful Adventures of Nils* is so far removed that, for the first time, reading makes me feel even drearier.

Life in *The Stamp from the Land of Gondeloupa* is the same as in Udelnaya, except that it's improbably easy, convenient, and not scary. The book appeals to me because it's about stamps. Only I refuse to believe the bit about a whole series fitting on one envelope. One of Papa's colleagues, when he left for the front, entrusted me with his precious 1937 *Yvert* stamp catalogue for the rest of the war. I discovered that a Swedish series consisted not of ten, but twelve stamps, none of them like the ones on the cover of *Gondeloupa*. *Yvert* worked miracles. Without a dictionary I understood much more than just the obvious *rouge, bleu, bistre,* and *vermillon*. I got stuck on the *timbres* in *timbres-poste* and on *guerre de l'independence* — because of the resemblance to *l'Inde*.

Le Chevalier de la Maison Rouge was my first grown-up novel, 365 pages. A sweet and secret ache made me realize that to tell Mama/Papa about the love of Maurice and Genevieve would be as unthinkable as telling them about *frucking*.

Kind Great Aunt Asya brought me sets of the children's monthly *Hedgehog* from the late '20s and early '30s, from Igor and Boris who had outgrown them. The grown-ups all skimmed and scanned *Hedgehog*, it never occurred to any of them that I might be better off without it — after all, they always turned the radio off at the mention of Pavlik Morozov. According to *Hedgehog*, life everywhere was loathsome. In America, for example. The only good person there was one of us, a Young Pioneer named Harry Eisman (see his letter and picture), everyone else was bad, not one of us. The *Pinkerton Agency* in *Hedgehog* bore no relation to the splendid Nat Pinkerton of Papa's recollections. A miserable out-of-work worker, he gets a job as a plainclothesman and goes from issue to issue — in the pictures — torturing and killing other workers like him. *Hedgehog* also had some funny things about silly inventions: a machine to pick apples, a machine to remove your boots, a machine to scrub your back. But *Hedgehog*'s chief concern was the League of Nations, cigar-smoking capitalists, and counterrevolutionary talks on disarmament. The fascists all looked like Americans: Italian fascists made you drink castor oil, German ones beat you.

While waiting for the Germans, *Hedgehog* went into the

stove. Papa's "agricultural" *Just an Ordinary Horse* by Shershe-nevich went in, too, by mistake. The stove stood warm from books for two days.

Anything of value — rings, watches, lengths of fabric, my stamps — we buried by the porch under the foundation. When we dug them up, the stamps had turned moldy and the pictures yellow from the homemade mounting squares that now showed through.

The Germans were supposed to arrive — in Udelnaya and in Moscow — on the 16th of October (1941). Everyone — in Moscow and in Udelnaya — somehow learned right away that a train carrying the government had left the metro.

Mama and I felt terrified alone in our dacha. We spent the night at a neighbor's.

Blue-eyed, gray-haired Mikhei — he had a tsarist fifty-kopeck piece and Crimean pebbles — was rushing furiously around the room:

"The first formation I see, I'll walk right through it and I'll say: 'Brothers!'"

His wife was sitting by the kettle:

"Yelnya, Yelnya, all this fuss about Yelnya! Why don't they write about my Rzhishchevo? Where's my mama now? Mikhei stop running around!"

Mikhei didn't stop:

"...and scurfy Yids all over the place! First they're here then they're there! Scurfy Yids!"

That night I asked Mama about the new word:

"Scurfy: is that because they scurry?"

I couldn't fall asleep for a long time, I kept remembering:

"Ich bin ein Schuler. Ich heisse Andrei. Mein Vater ist Sergeev. Meine Mutter ist Mikhailova. Wir sind russisch."

The year before, at Bolshaya Ekaterininskaya Street, Granny's Czech acquaintance, the music teacher Alexander Schwarz, had learned of my passion for France, and disapproved:

"I went all through Europe with German. Learn German and everyone will understand you."

Mama taught me a little of the German she had taken away with her from her gymnasium.

"That time when we were waitin' for the Germans, I remember I kept pacin' back and forth callin' up German phrases, I thought I'd start right in speakin' German with 'em. Then it dawned on me: they'll just march me off to headquarters and make me translate. And they'll take Andrei, hook him with a bayonet. No, I thought, better keep quiet."

In the morning we went home to bed. Suddenly, across the Makedonka, a cannonade began. Mama leapt up, fell and banged her shins hard on the iron frame of her cot. Groaning, she gave the key another turn in the lock and drew the curtains more tightly. It seemed even more frightening to go to the shelter. In Moscow, Granny and Grandfather never went to any shelter: fate.

Towards evening it began to quiet down. Mama peeked out through the glass door onto the veranda: on the wooden trestle-bed, his face hidden, a strange, fat soldier slept.

When he woke up, he turned out to be a Red Army man, Aleksei Ivanovich. He explained that on the other side of the river, in Novaya Malakhovka, an ordnance depot had exploded.

Aleksei Ivanovich took to coming by, either by himself, or with women. He crooned:

> Life ain't worth livin'
> Without its delights.

Shurka and I nicknamed him Cachalot.

Cachalot would drink then suddenly start screaming that all military men were parasites. He brought us canned food and suet from the depot in exchange for our last apples/plums. His wife came out from Moscow and cried, she brought him textiles from the shop to sell.

Everyone was grabbing everything they could. On someone's advice Mama and I set off for a rabbit farm beyond Chudakovo. There, for free — because Papa was an old friend — they gave us two pullovers from the showcase: what a beautiful sight — one white, the other blue-and-white striped like a s a i l o r ' s v e s t. I couldn't wear either: the down got in my mouth.

Papa himself relieved the House of Agronomists of a thoroughly dusty collection of minerals, a dummy F-1 grenade, and a school microscope twisted out of shape. He also carried off the volumes that were missing from our *Small Soviet Encyclopedia*.

After the sixteenth of October, Papa came out to fetch us. The electric suburban trains weren't running. Between the station platform and the platform of the steam-train a chasm yawned. Mama jumped across it, Papa followed with me in his arms.

At Kazan Station a lone Red Army man with a rifle stood by the exit checking internal passports. Outside the station there were lots of women sitting on bundles.

On First Meshchanskaya Street we saw refugees trudging after horse-drawn carts. One of the carts was piled with the remains of a plywood fighter plane.

At the tram stop, men in mustard-green great coats and square military hats, apparently Poles, are talking among themselves in unthinkably obscene Russian.

First Meshchanskaya, by Samgina's Gymnasium, is lined with American S t u d e b a k e r s.

In a stamp store on Kuznetsky Most an officer of neutral Bulgaria is buying up rarities from who knows where.

The rare edition bookshops are crammed with magnificent old volumes. The jewelers' and even the notions shops are full of semi-precious stones. A beautiful stone the size of a nut costs the same as two or three kilos of potatoes.

Twice there's been an air-raid warning. Anti-aircraft fired from near the Central House of the Red Army. The Red Army Theater has been camouflaged with patches of paint; a lean-to tacked onto the front of it is meant to disguise its pentagonal shape and make it look like a church from the air. The square in front of the theater is full of anti-aircraft with monitors.

In our roomy Udelnaya dacha the anti-aircraft fire made you drunk. You wanted to hang out the window and watch. On Kapelsky Lane, in our cramped upstairs quarters, I didn't want to go near the windows. Not out of a sense of danger — I never had that.

Mama had gotten in line at the bakery opposite the local post office, No. 110, I was waiting on the corner. I had been there maybe ten minutes when I suddenly saw an unhinged trolleybus coming right for me. Unafraid, unsurprised, I moved out of the way. The trolleybus crashed, the bakery shook. Passers-by reassured Mama:

"There was a boy standing there, but he ran away."

I didn't run, I walked.

At the market, a kilo of potatoes costs between 70 and 80 rubles, a kilo of sugar between 700 and 800 rubles, a kilo of butter between 1,000 and 1,200. Our ration cards — plus Granny/ Grandfather's — give us a lot of bread. One evening in the bakery, Papa hawks a loaf of black bread for 120 rubles right off the bat.

Wondrous foods appear: sesame oil in the shops and *cocoavella* in office cafeterias.

For New Year's we are issued two hundred grams of *Siberia* caramels with the little squirrel on the wrapper.

New wartime things. For the cold: a chemical hot-water bottle. A thick paper bag you have to fill with hot water, then its weak warmth lasts a long time.

For the darkness (to keep people from knocking into each other outside): a badge. Either a luminous daisy or a plain paper circle set in tin.

In winter the houses weren't heated, often there was no electricity. In the dark of our communal kitchen, Tonka poured a large pot of precious potatoes down my back. I screamed and screamed. The next thing I remember, I'm on my trestle bed, in our room, and all the neighbors are coming by with bottles. My back is being treated with compresses of sunflower oil. No one grudged me theirs. When the ambulance arrived, the doctor said: second-degree burn; there's nothing more to do, everything's already been done.

Amazed and nonplussed, I come across Papa's copies of Mayakovsky's *A Cloud in Pants* and Erenburg's *Julio Jurenito*. I learn both by heart. From them it's clear that there were, are, and will surely be other, vibrant countries, another, vibrant life. That first winter of the war I came to know and love the brisk, bright word *Futurism*.

I couldn't believe that Erenburg was the same Erenburg who wrote articles in the papers about little Hitler putting tacks on his nanny's chair.

The food shops are empty, their windows filled with TASS propaganda posters:

> Little Fritz, that naughty boy,
> Strung up cats, then looked coy.

> As for the Nazi who told the peasant,
> Off with your hat, you excrescence!
> Partisans soon cut off his head
> Since fascists look better dead.

> Hitler's on the fence
> And making a hash of things,
> To keep his mangy men
> From completely starving.

A riddle on a tear-off calendar:

> What's absolutely vile and begins with an H?
> (Hitler — written upside down)

In the paper:

> Horty, Ryti, Antonescu,
> Nedic, Quisling and Laval.

In the paper, back from oblivion, the once all-powerful lickspittle Demyan Bedny, alias Efim Pridvorov, has crawled out for all to see — he's either the son of a grand duke, or a Jew. From his *Komsomol Easter* I had at some point picked up:

> Deacon Kir cuffs the priest Afanasy...
> Evpl, Khuzdazat, Turvon, Lupp,
> Evksakostudian, Proskudia, Kozdoya.

Granny/Mama did not approve of my having read *Komsomol Easter*. But then I found something just as biting in *Pravda*:

A Berlin night in a blizzard:
Goebbels' sensitive innards
Are balking at an untimely end.
That's why it is that then
Goebbels at his bomb-shelter desk
Felt so down and depressed:
The night before Christmas
With no cheer or jolliness,
With no boasts of a victory jamboree.
Down in the dumps,
Taking his lumps,
He dictated to his secretary...

The development of transportation today did not save us. Papa and Granny had to go from fifty to a hundred kilometers away to trade things, mostly for potatoes. The s i c k l y - s w e e t half-frozen ones went into fritters; the unfrozen ones, practically unpeeled, we boiled or fried in water.

In Taldom a woman promised Papa all kinds of things, took the length of material and disappeared. Papa didn't despair, he still thought it paid to trust people. Mama nagged:

"You always do that..."

Granny trusted no one when bartering, especially now there were swindlers everywhere... She could spot where the sunflower oil ended in a bottle and — halfway down — the urine began.

Mama and I had made our way in town. Our tram was crawling from Trubnaya Square to Petrovskiye Vorota. By the exit, a woman suddenly started screaming: her purse had been picked and she had the thief by the arm. It was the usual, wartime crush. The other passengers couldn't pretend not to notice so they — men and women — bundled the young, wild-eyed thief down onto the pavement.

"Stop twisting my arm! That hurts! I'll go myself!" the thief screamed at the policemen who had turned up from somewhere. Passengers thronged behind. A black, important-looking motorcar slowly skirted the crowd. One bound — and the thief was hanging onto the rear grille. The rest is like a film in slow motion: the motorcar lurches, the grille bends slowly back, and the thief is thrown down onto the pavement and dragged for another ten or twenty meters on his knees, leaving dark streaks.

Hunger: in Little Pines a dog sniffs its own freshly produced shit, then sets about neatly eating it.

No one made any preparations for the first winter of the war.

Desultory preparations for the second winter were begun in early spring. On the advice of the papers/radio, people cut off the tops of tubers and grew the seeds. We dug up most of the yard for a kitchen garden, and we let some distant acquaintances stay in the house — we never had any close ones.

Uncle Ivan prowled his half of the property by night with a Berdan rifle.

Mama's feuds with his wife Avdotia had been forgotten and I was often left to guard our half of the dacha alone. Avdotia, that w i t c h, that h a r r i d a n, that c a r p y h a r p y, Mama's talk of the town, loaned me library editions of Leskov, Tyutchev, Stanyukovich, Alexander Grin, and a book about Pushkin's friends.

The peace with her lasted through the war.

Through the war and after I kept a journal. I made a notepad out of letterhead:

MOSCOW Region AGRONOMISTS' CLUB
Dolgoprudnaya P.O., Krasnopolyansk Dist., Moscow Region
...............194..
9 June 1944

I'm living at the dacha.
Mama brought me a journal today so I can record what has
happened since 21 May when we came to Udelnaya. My
kitchen garden is small: altogether I've planted potatoes
(9 pcs.), tomatoes (10 pcs.), peas (25 pcs.), beans
(8 pcs.), corn (15 pcs.), French beans (3 pcs.).
Everything has come up except the beans...

19 July 1945

As soon as I opened the veranda door I saw maybe 10 boys
go tearing out of the strawberry patch and make for the gate.
The lock on the gate was broken. Of course I was scared.

It's terrifying to see a lot of strange backs hustling towards the
gate. Terrifying to be alone at the dacha. Luckily, Papa has boarded
up the glass veranda doors. Unluckily, the windows are so large
and low that anyone going by can see in. Glass is no protection.

Shurka Morozov — the garden robber — wouldn't leave me
alone, and not because he could eat anything out of our garden.
The reason was stamps, coins, toy soldiers, and games.

Sitting in the attic, we thought up marching orders, drew
maps, invented medals. I cut them out of tin cans with pruning
shears and colored them with oil paint.

At the table in the garden we played cards, just the two of us,
with d u m m i e s .

We confabulated in a secret language of school-gutter origin.
Instead of I *want a smoke*:

"I-honsee wa-honsee a-honsee smo-honsee."

We smoked awful cherry leaves, straw, and occasionally low-grade tobacco or crummy fags with cardboard mouthpieces: *Nord*, *Putina*, *Priboi*. Before the war, I filched a cheap *Raketa* from Grandfather — just to try.

Shurka's profanity dazzled. In response to the request, "Leave me some":

"Get fucked by a measly Tatar." Or:

"Stick yer prick in a bag so the cookies don't crumble!" Or:

"Have a smoke, soon you'll croak, and I'll get all yer stuff."

His idea of wit: 'Wanna trade?"

"?"

"My dick in yer mouth for yer tongue in my ass!"

Shurka would jump free of conductors at full speed, after picking up all kinds of suburban train lilts:

> In a sunny southern clime,
> Where the winds don't whine,
> There lived a handsome Latin,
> A jungle-mad Italian...

> Vasenka pushed me first, yes-yes,
> My stomach nearly burst, yes-yes,
> So I forgot about fear,
> Pulled Vasenka by the ear,
> And sent the poor boy flying.

> Insulted Kostya wouldn't stand for it,
> The blood went rushing to his face,
> He pulled a knife out of his pocket,
> And plunged it in the fatal place.

Sitting on the roof one day,
Maybe higher, who's to say,
Maybe even on the stovepipe...

All summer long I lolled on the roof — we had no lodgers so the upstairs was unoccupied — bawling songs and arias. Garden robbers raced down the lane, bellowing:

"Andrei, sing us a serenade!"

I always waited for Shurka's triple-whistle signal: I was afraid to go to his house by myself, I felt uneasy outside my gate, terrified that Shurka's dog Mukhtarka might bite me — once she did.

Shurka liked to announce himself:

Home sweet home is it!
Smells of hay and shit!

With Shurka I didn't feel scared: we went bathing. Shurka was an excellent swimmer, I could barely keep afloat. The bubble of air in my roomy, wet, black sateen underpants held me up.

Once we tried to string up a kitten: we remembered how *little Fritz, that naughty boy, strung up cats...* We prepared a shoelace, chose a branch — then broke down and let the kitten go.

Another time we went sailing down the narrow Makedonka on a raft, stirring up the water by the small wooden docks. A woman rinsing laundry scolded us. Shurka: "Shut up, hag!"

"How dare you talk to me like that, I'm old enough to be your mother!"

"You're not good enough to shine my shoes!"

Well-meaning neighbors whispered to Mama:

"What can Andrei have in common with that ruffian?"

To say the same about Yurka Tikhonov wouldn't have occurred to them: he came from a nice family.

The Tikhonovs came from Kapelsky Lane. When Yurka was born, my father traded his roomy semi-basement on Pokrovka Street for their small, upstairs room on Kapelsky.

Yurka's habit of spying earned him the nickname Spook: a mortal insult. With me he was always very high-hat: the four-year age difference and his Moscow street experience. He called me a singleton.

He reasoned: "Because because

         Ends with an E."

He agreed pompously: "It's a fact."

   playfully: "You're right, you owe me a ruble."

   jovially: "You're right, Arkashka, your ass is fatter."

   farting: "My ass confirms it."

He reasoned: "And you call that swimming..."

He summed up: " 'Mustn't overdo a good thing'," said the old woman, crawling out from under a bus."

He refused: "So take that!" pointing to his fly.

In disapproving of Shurka, the neighbors didn't notice that while one was as outrageous, say, as the other, Shurka's folklore was boyish and hale, whereas Yurka's was grown-up and tired:

> The major wants,
> The madam taunts...
>
> On the island of Tahiti
> Lived big black Titi-Iti...
>
> In Capetown port,
> With cocoa on board,
> The *Jeannetta* was setting sail...

If Yurka had a new one, then often as not it was God forbid:

> An old woman made her way
> Slowly 'cross the highway,
> She was stopped by a surly policeman:
> "You didn't hear me talking!
> I caught you jaywalking!
> Grandma, I say, you gotta pay the fine!"
> "Oi, what am I to do,
> But then to hell with you!
> My Jacob's home with nothing to do —
> I'm bringing him these buns,
> Some delicious cold tongue,
> Pies and a small piece of chicken for lunch.
> I won't give you a crumb,
> Jacob will eat the sum,
> He'll stuff himself till he's taut as a drum..."

> "Vasya, Vasya, why so blue?
> What on earth is troubling you?
> Or has Jacob the baker
> Gone again and cheated you?"
> "Charged me for ten loaves of bread,
> But gave me five instead
> As soon as I see him,
> Jacob is as good as dead!"

Yurka lured me with a greasy ledger full of stamps: the Straits Settlement, Labuan, Abyssinia, a blue American one:

"Lincoln, he freed the Negroes."

In a round cardboard sweetmeat box, he kept coins:

"Platinum, the lightest metal there is," Yurka was showing me an aluminum League of Nations token.

On a very heavy coin, as I now recall, though I know I'm wrong:

3 SILVER RUBLES 1840 — and around the circumference: PURE URALS PLATINUM.

(According to *Krause*, there is only one 1840 platinum three-ruble coin in existence in the world, and the inscription is right).

Yurka wouldn't part with either the light token or the heavy coin. Once I heard him hum:

"My finances are singing romances. Take a Catherine II ruble. It'll cost you seventy."

The price was astronomical and to be taken for a fool humiliating. I turned the Catherine rubles over and over until I read on the best one:

PETER III G.G. EMP. AND SOV. ALLRUS.

I took it. The money came from my kitchen garden, the price of a kilo of tomatoes. I'd grown them myself and sold them myself to lodgers living next-door.

In time, more and more of the surplus from the orchard/kitchen garden went to market. Avdotia sold what she had herself. Mama never: she sent either Granny or Anna Aleksandrovna, the Tikhonovs' nun:

> "Apples, sourer than sass,
> Line right up, working class!"

After market, they counted the proceeds: I watched as unwonted bills — issued in the '30s and then withdrawn — cropped up from who knew where. Oddly enough, people accepted these dubious notes as readily as the one-ruble bill with the miner, the three-ruble bill with the Red Army man, the five-ruble bill with the pilot, and the ten-ruble bill with Lenin.

Anna Aleksandrovna had a silver Nicholas II ruble. She considered it was worth as much as she could buy with it at the time. I made my peace with the fact that it would never be mine.

Anna Aleksandrovna (Mama called her S a i n t behind her back) came from the formerly privileged classes and had been at the Belomor-Baltic labor camp, as a convict. The Tikhonovs let her live in their dacha one winter as caretaker: she stayed on and set up a small convent for others like herself. From morning till night, old women shuffled from the station and the Udelnaya church to the Tikhonovs' and back. Either because no one bothered to inform or because it was wartime, they were left alone. The neighbors called Anna Aleksandrovna Holier-Than-Thou and would have been glad to say bad things about her. She thought we were all of us Reds. Whatever she did or said, it smacked of defiance and suspicion.

"Hello to you. Can you spare any chickweed?"

"Help yourself!" Papa always said.

Under the apple trees in front of our veranda she would pick chickweed for her hen. I would fidget nearby and she would start talking to me, always about her own affairs. She had loaned me an old — pre-revolutionary — translation from French for the summer.

Journal:

19 June 1945

Anna Aleksandrovna gave me *Sermons for Children* by De Cauppette to read. It's a wonderful book.

Those simple little stories made me weep, I kept quiet about my tears and about my impressions. One passage I never forgot. I sang it to a melody that I had made up:

> I will wait upon thee: for God is my defense, and I will
> sing of thy power; yea, I will sing aloud of thy mercy in the
> morning: for thou hast been my defense and refuge in the day
> of my trouble.

Thirty years later or more I learned that it came from the Fifty-Ninth Psalm.

I started second grade again in Udelnaya.

Refugees appeared. The ones from Leningrad were settled in a deserted village once inhabited — long before the war — by former tsarist convicts.

It didn't occur to the Leningraders to tell us about the Seige, any more than it did to us to ask them.

Refugees from outside Moscow lived wherever. One of them had the wildly dangerous nickname Hitler's Herdsman. He must have grazed his cow on German-occupied territory.

Nicknames were equally popular — in Udelnaya, in Moscow — everywhere:

> Gray: a fair-haired boy (respected)
> Mouse: a fair-haired boy (small)
> Sage (the herb): a swarthy boy (usually a Tatar)
> Mora: a gypsy-like boy (I'm Mora from the chorus)
> Chinesy: a Mongolian-looking boy
> Worms: tall and thin
> Ruble-Forty or Two-and-a-Half or Three-Rubles: lame
> Paper Cone: ephemeral
> Fatya: fat (after the comic Fatty Arbuckle)
> Kotovsky: bald or crew cut
> Vovochkin: an obsequious diminutive of Vladimir
> Kolyá: a devil-may-care diminutive of Nikolai

The German Yiddish last name Wieseltier, marvelous to the Russian ear, precluded any adaptation or replacement with a nickname since it already sounded like a tsarist sobriquet: "I say, Wieseltier!"

Toucan was a nickname, too: the vice-principal's nose resembled the bill of this tropical bird. Classmates claimed Toucan had gone into the girls' outhouse after our teacher Lydia Stepanovna and peed in her ass. Because of this, Lydia Stepanovna had produced two little girls.

I felt comfortable in the Udelnaya school: I learned my lessons and kept to myself. Shurka Morozov had it worse, being from Udelnaya, a known quantity, and marked to boot: the ringworm from the station barber's had worked on the crown of his head. Bald spot: is that one word or two?

When they ganged up on him, he was always ready to fight back — and, trumpeting, would yell:

"Better to fart like a man than shit like a chicken!" and finish with a flourish: "Friend, have a sniff, of my yeasty whiff."

Besides Shurka and me, no one cared much about stamps/ coins. We would dig up stamps — dark blue tsarist 7-kopeck ones and light blue French 15-centime ones — and pass them around for free in little stacks of a hundred tied with time-yellowed thread.

In second grade I suffered my first pangs of conscience. A sweet and cultivated boy from Moscow named Igor showed me his coins. During the long recess, when there was no one in the classroom — everyone was running around outside — I sat down at his desk, raised the lid and took out his collection — I wanted to have another look. Then I decided to play a trick and stuffed the coins in my pocket — Igor would find them gone and look scared,

I'd laugh and give them back. I even told the girl sitting next to me about my plan, but she didn't pay any attention.

I was judging by myself — if anything of mine were to disappear, I would immediately complain to a good friend. But Igor was self-possessed and well brought up, he kept quiet and behaved as if nothing had happened, so I had no occasion to return the coins.

Thus I became a self-acknowledged thief. How those coins chafed — the Austrian kreutzer, the American nickel with the bison, the Polish two-zloty piece with the young lady, plus a dozen worthless Russian, Latvian, Estonian, and Lithuanian coppers. I could throw them away, but it wouldn't spare me the anguish. I could return them, but it was too disgracefully late. So I sat on my stolen goods — worth next to nothing at the time and not much more now.

Before November 7th — the twenty-fifth anniversary of the *Revolushit*— they began getting our class ready for the celebration.

Among ourselves, we sang only irreverent versions of Soviet songs. Now a Young Pioneer leader, a girl, tried to drum the official texts into our heads:

> Our armour is strong, our tanks are fast...

> Fight for the Motherland, fight for Stalin,
> Our battle honor is dear to us.
> Our sturdy steeds are champing at the bit,
> We'll meet our foe as Stalin would.

> Our tread is steadier,
> No enemy will ever,
> Walk through these republics of ours!

In 1942 this was an impossible song to sing, and I grumbled to myself:

> Our tread is steadier,
> The enemy will ever
> Walk through these republics of ours!

Still, when they asked who wanted to introduce the class and announce the song, I volunteered. At home, when my head had cleared, I suddenly felt uncertain and afraid.

We returned to Moscow before the November holidays. I was spared the embarrassment of the celebration and, most of all, my unbearable shame before Igor. My shame before myself remained.

THE COMMUNAL APARTMENT

Once as we were leaving Udelnaya for Moscow — this was before the war — Papa told me that I must say hello to everyone in the apartment on our return, and every day after that.

I was showing the kitchen the cover of a new *Murzilka*:
"Who does that look like?"
In the color frame, a towering Mayakovsky was bent almost in half as he chatted gloomily with a little girl on Red Square.
"Like Alimpy!" the whole kitchen cried.
At seven, I was firmly mired in the gossip about our strange neighbor Alimpy. Only recently he'd been running about with a French passport, but then he'd had to exchange it for a regular one. He was not like normal people, he didn't notice his neighbors, never said hello, he sat in the WC for an hour at a time or, on the contrary, might lock someone else in, he rushed up and down the corridor like a madman — if you didn't look out, he'd knock you off your feet or the frying pan out of your hands. It irritated the kitchen that he changed his muffler so often and wore wide-brim checked-cloth caps made to order:
"Just like Mayakovsky's."

Alimpy was the son of the Bernardessa — in peacetime the entire apartment had belonged to them — four smallish rooms, a kitchen with an adjoining maid's room, a bath and a WC. Their remnants of the former luxury consisted in a toilet bowl with a sky blue English lion on it and a meter with the legend SIEMENS-SCHUCKERT.
Before Kapelsky Lane, the Bernards had lived even better:
"When Louis was alive we rented an apartment near Sretenskiye Vorota in the Rossia insurance building."

The French Bernardessa spoke, like Maly Theater actors, in the old Moscow manner. In her decadent idiom, the WC was the *vater*.

It was from her I first heard the age-old:

> Chizhik-Pyzhik where've you been?
> On Fontanka drinking gin.

She remembered another rhyme in the same vein:

> A wee little chap
> Got up on a chair
> Took off his cap:
> No change to spare?

I readily identified myself with the wee little chap.

During the war, hungry children — neighborhood diplomats — would ring our front doorbell:

"Does the old French lady live here?"

At those sweet sounds the Bernardessa would drag herself out of her room with a stale sweetmeat or a discolored candy.

She had been a prostitute once. Then she married the man of affairs Ludvig Bernard — it was he who called himself Louis and had French citizenship. All their most personal possessions — letters with stamps, picture postcards, the passe-partout around framed photographs — were Austro-Hungarian: Bernhardt.

The kitchen whispered that while building the Nirnzee house, workmen had pushed Louis the man of affairs off the scaffolding.

In a slim volume about old Moscow, neighbors discovered a picture of the Bernardessa's father, police inspector Raskind. According to the author, police inspector Raskind had fleeced dossers at the Khitrov Market.

Mama hinted that Granny's brother, Great Uncle Semyon,

also a man of affairs, had given Raskind bribes: in *Tryokhgorny Lane*, in the back rooms, Great Uncle Semyon had an illegal (during the war?) baccarat.

The Bernardessa was visited by her sister, the unhappy Augusta, a mummified old maid — just like the Englishwoman in Chekhov.

The Bernardessa was visited by her brother Sasha Raskind, a one-time nepman and man of affairs still, a doer of shady deals according to the kitchen. Once he found me with a Napoleon III five-centime piece:

"Foreign currency!"

As a man of affairs he was, evidently, useless. All through the war there was talk of how he had gone bankrupt paying interest to an illicit money-lender and how r i c h Yulka had refused to bail him out.

The Bernardessa had the best room in the apartment while her son Alimpy and his Byelorussian wife wound up in the tiny maid's room off the kitchen. The old woman rarely rose from her bed:

"Gout..."

Gout was a noble disease, from champagne. The consensus in the kitchen was that her gout was syphilis, but that didn't make anyone squeamish. They only grumbled when the Bernardessa had been sitting in the vater for an hour. At night she excreted trumpeting sounds for the whole apartment to hear:

"She's shooting," the kitchen snickered.

From time to time a court physician, Doctor Taubkin, would come round to see the Bernardessa. In front of the neighbors or on the telephone he was:

"Professor Taubkin."

Over several winters during the war, simple-minded Vanechka — small, slight, age indeterminate — would often slip in to see her. He begged by a church, the neighbors made fun of him, then he was run over by a tram.

Several times a year the Bernardessa would ask Mama: "Did you know that the Virgin was Jewish?"

Under the Bernardessa's pillow lay smothered with kisses:

a carte-postale of the Vladimir Virgin,

a wooden, palm-sized Saint Nicholas,

a small, oval, enameled icon of Tryphon the Martyr.

The purity of the icon's colors kindled my imagination: I was starved for brightness. Ekaterina Dmitrievna, a chorus singer at the *Nemirovich*, gave me the shiny red tag from a pair of American stockings — I couldn't take my eyes off it.

The Bernardessa had rare treasures unlike those of anyone else in the apartment. In a locked bookcase behind curtained panes:

a gilt-edged 19th-century Wolf edition of *Grimms' Fairy Tales*;

sets of cinema newspapers from the '20s;

a wooden coffee mill with a spring handle and sliding drawer;

an antique locomotive equipped with a cannon.

Strictly speaking, all this belonged to Alimpy and was meant for him alone.

Despite the taboo, the Bernardessa loaned me *Grimms'*; Tonka, Alimpy's wife, trusted me for extended periods with the cinema newspapers; and coffee was constantly being ground in the coffee mill.

Sometimes Alimpy would shut himself up in the big room and run the locomotive on the table — the locomotive was supposed to run on rails and whistle softly. I myself never saw it.

In the corridor above the coat-rack, instead of hats, and below the coat-rack, instead of galoshes, lay Alimpy's old school books, incidental books, and little albums with color drawings of film stars: Runich, Maksimov, Polonsky. No one kept an eye on these books so — one by one — Mama smuggled *History of the Ancient World*, *Geography of the Russian Empire*, and Hemingway's *A Farewell to Arms* into our room for me.

The Bernardessa's sons had creative temperaments.

The younger son, Yuli, a disfranchised person barred from university study, married the weak-sighted widow of the r i c h actor Kuznetsov and went to work as an assistant director at the Maly Theater. Sometimes one came across *Stage manager Yu. Bernard* in the program.

Yuli's w e l l b r o u g h t u p stepson, Kuznetsov's son Misha, stunned me with his crudely sober view of life:

> When they give: grab,
> When they hit: skip.

We read in *Murzilka*:

> That lamp is mine, I swear,
> This inkwell, too, so there!

"Greedy-guts," Misha concluded.

I delighted in plays on words, in sounds and assonances, it didn't occur to me that from verses one could elicit — in one word — the essence. I pondered: the essence turned out to be true, but not mine.

The elder son, Alimpy, managed to complete a few years of gymnasium and knew that he had ideas, taste and manners.

He spent his Sundays preparing to go out: he would clean his boots and lapels, call his friend the manager of the Forum cinema, order two box seats, and take Tonka out after lunch to see something foreign.

Alimpy listened earnestly to the radio: to play readings from the Moscow Art Theater, the Maly, and the Leninsky Komsomol Theater; to stand-up comedians; to light opera arrangements; and most of all — the late '30s and early '40s saw a genuine flowering — to radio musicals and radio plays.

Through the constantly open door of the big room you could see him standing there in some uncomfortable position for hours, transfixed by the black paper loudspeaker bellowing for the whole apartment to hear.

His idol was the actor Terekhov, so extraordinarily good-looking that Mama suspected him:

"All Jewish men are handsome..."

And on this celebrated Terekhov, supplier Alimpy contrived to press an invitation. While Terekhov was taking off his galoshes in the front hall, Mama just had time to show him a set of postcards — from the '20s, of Terekhov in various roles. And the guest just had time to ooh and ah — he didn't have any of these postcards himself — before Alimpy, with an ostentatious gesture, showed him into his room.

Terekhov had come by after a performance, late, when, in the opinion of the kitchen, the guests waiting to meet Terekhov had already eaten everything. For days afterwards the wives couldn't get over it:

"He arrives, and what do they give him, a pear on a plate."

"They'd probably had that pear a month, been keeping it for him, completely rotten."

Alimpy was not liked, or rather, notliked, one word.

The kitchen suspected him of all kinds of terrible things because of his friendship with a chauffeur from the American Embassy: normal people were afraid to have anything to do with embassy types;

they accused him of breeding bedbugs; the bedbugs came from the bedridden Bernardessa; during the worst winter I killed over a hundred in one night;

they fumed about his Moscow Anti-aircraft Defense service — it saved him from the front.

Once Mama, forgetting herself, called to him:

"Alimpy Ludvigovich, you're wanted on the telephone!" — and then froze: rumor had it that the half-witted Alimpy could hit you.

As a child Valentin Ludvigovich Bernard had called himself Alya — and over the years Alya had turned into the grown-up Alimpy.

For all their animosity, the neighbors vied with each other to try and get him to talk to them, and boasted if he deigned to reply.

Alimpy was the only one in the apartment — perhaps in the neighborhood — who read the supple, magic-scented, postwar magazine *America*. *America* blazed with the summer-fall heat in all the kiosks: expensive (10 rubles) and scary (buy it, but then what if...?)

That longed-for, marvelous, magnificent magazine came to me through Tonka, and I reveled in the otherness of the existence pictured there — it was all so bright and unlike mine:

Sandburg's poems,

Wyeth's paintings,

artistic photography,

modern cities with brightly dressed crowds,

an ultramarine farmer by his vermilion tractor,
the marvelous, clean lines and solid colors of pots and pans...

Mama — when I was maybe fourteen — invited Alimpy to listen to two Vertinsky records I had on loan. He declined to come into our room and, suffering, listened from the corridor.

He was oddly tactful.

He never borrowed anything from anyone.

He didn't notice sidelong glances.

After he had finished in the WC, he would burn the piece of paper he had wiped himself with — actually, so would Klara Ivanovna and Boris Fyodorovich, Aleksei Semyonovich and Ekaterina Dmitrievna. After the Bernardessa, it always smelled for a long time of an old woman's fustiness.

In the summer of '53, we moved to Chapayev Lane. Alimpy died soon after. Before the war he had been maybe thirty-five.

In our communal apartment on Kapelsky there was not one person

who had been decorated,

not one Party member,

not one military man,

not one engineer,

no one was ever arrested,

no one evacuated,

no one was sent to the front: Boris Fyodorovich and Papa because of their age, Aleksei Semyonovich because of an exemption, Alimpy because of his alternative service (due to poor health, I imagine).

I myself don't come into these calculations: underage.

The grown-ups could be paired off according to particular attributes (excluding family ones) — two by two:

Russians: Papa and Mama,
Ukrainians: Aleksei Semyonovich and Ekaterina Dmitrievna,
other Slavs: Boris Fyodorovich and Tonka,
would-be Balts: Boris Fyodorovich and Klara Ivanovna,
Jews: the Bernardessa and Alimpy,
former foreign subjects: idem,
former prostitutes: the Bernardessa and Klara Ivanovna,
from the formerly privileged classes: Boris Fyodorovich and
the Bernardessa,
Candidates of Science: Papa and Aleksei Semyonovich,
artistic temperaments: Alimpy and Ekaterina Dmitrievna,
members of the intelligentsia: Boris Fyodorovich and Aleksei
Semyonovich,
office workers: Boris Fyodorovich and Tonka,
teachers: Papa and Aleksei Semyonovich,
old and pensionless: the Bernardessa and Boris Fyodorovich,
attended gymnasium: Mama and Alimpy,
never went to school: Klara Ivanovna and Tonka,
caused rows: idem,
got on everyone's nerves: the Bernardessa and Aleksei
Semyonovich,
frightened you: Alimpy and Aleksei Semyonovich.

The kitchen was a People's Assembly, Comrades' Court, telegraph agency, discussion club and self-service theater rolled into one.

The minute I was born, the kitchen demanded that I be assigned a regular cleaning quota, like anyone else in the apartment, and that Mama do mine for me — Mama always payed Klara Ivanovna or Nyusha the milkmaid to do that for her.

In the kitchen, dramas such as *using someone else's burner* or *not writing down how much gas one had used* were acted out just for the hell of it.

The kitchen had its own expressions (*old fart, cuckoofart, superbsky*), its own stock phrases (e.g. *painted ladies are popping up* — always in reference to the Bernardessa), its own favorite rhymes (Mikhalkov's fable *The Fox and the Beaver*), its own riddle about the tram:

> One man drives,
> Another barks,
> Ten bigwigs sit there like kings,
> Ninety stand packed like sardines,
> Daredevils hang from the railings,
> Two hundred with envy turn green.

And its own jokes — n o t   d a n g e r o u s ones:

"A general's wife is boasting about her new piano. 'But it has no resonance,' her listener objects. 'Doesn't matter,' she says. 'My Vanya will buy everything it needs. He'll buy a resonance, too.' "

"A woman dressed to the nines flounces down the street past a man lying unconscious on the sidewalk. 'What a knockout!' passers-by remark. 'Oh, I didn't knock him out,' she says, 'my husband did.'"

" 'I'm swapping my forty-year-old wife for two twenty-year-olds!' "

" 'I'm swapping my wife for a room in a communal apartment!' "

"In wartime a foreigner turns up at the Moscow baths. On his way in he's given a small cake of soap — you know what kind? 'What's this?' he asks. 'It's good nut soap,' they tell him. 'But, you see,' he says meekly. 'I need to wash all of me.' "

"Roosevelt and Churchill say to Stalin: 'We've helped you out, so after the war you give us the Crimea.' Stalin says: 'Fine. Only guess which finger is the most important.' He shows them his thumb, forefinger and middle finger. Roosevelt thinks: 'Your middle finger because it's the longest.' Churchill thinks: 'Your thumb because it's the strongest.' 'You guessed it!' says Stalin, thumbing his nose and giving them the finger."

Ekaterina Dmitrievna told me quietly, s o   K l a r a   I v a n o v n a   w o u l d n ' t   h e a r:

"After the war they'll open new theaters in Moscow. At the Kalinin Theater they'll stage *A Servant of Two Masters*, at the Stalin Theater *Stay in your Own Lane*, and at the People's Theater *Guilty Without Guilt*."

I never heard a single joke from Klara Ivanovna, even one that wasn't dangerous: she liked to retail "s a t a i r i c a l" pieces from the papers.

The kitchen had its own public opinion.

It fearlessly expressed its disappointment in the new Soviet anthem. Unlike *God Save the Tsar*, it was a tiresome song: *O Party of Lenin, O Party of Stalin, Wise party of the Bolsheviks*. The *Internationale* was at least beautiful.

The kitchen took part in the general rivalry between tenors Lemeshev and Kozlovsky. It hadn't favored either until Kozlovsky himself made the fatal mistake of singing the role of the Holy Fool in *Boris Godunov*. The kitchen gasped: "He's sunk to that!"

During operas broadcast live from the Bolshoi, the kitchen made wisecracks and gloated over the prompter's audible whispers.

Specially for the kitchen, broadcasts featured arias from works that were cultural and comprehensible:

> *The Queen of Spades*
> *Lohengrin*
> *Eugene Onegin*

The Demon

Der Zigeunerbaron

L'elisir d'amore

Ruslan and Ludmila

Faust

The Barber of Seville

Boris Godunov

Sadko

The Pearl Fishers

La Prichole

The Marriage of Figaro

Silva

Rusalka

Carmen

Iolanta

The Hovansky Affair

Arshin Mal-Alan

and so as not to be outdone by sunny Georgia:

Keto and Kote (a musical comedy)

The obligatory line-up: composers Khrennikov; Budashkin; Gomolyaka; Meitus; Podkovyrov; Brusilovsky; Ryauzov; the Karelian-Finnish composer Pergament; Sirkka Rikka; Irma Yaunzem; the All-Union Radio Committee trio of accordion players (Kuznetsov, Popkov and Danilov); the Komitas Quartet; and another quartet: Zhuk, Veltman, Gurvich and Guravsky, all on violin — so tedious, just wears you out.

Fireworks to celebrate the taking of a city were invariably followed by an overture and concert by "masters of the art":

Kozlovsky

Lemeshev

Mikhailov

Pirogov

Reizen

Aleksei Ivanov

Andrei Ivanov

Petrov

Nelepp

Nortsov

Burlak

Maksakova

Preobrazhenskaya

Shpiller

Barsova

Pantofel-Nechetskaya

Shumskaya

Irina Maslennikova

Leokadia Maslennikova

Khromchenko

Orfyonov

Aleksandrovich

Bunchikov

Lebedeva and Kachalov

On holidays there were variety shows with comedians and songs by Soviet composers. On the Eve of either 1944 or 1945, the radio had the tactlessness to play something called *Artillery Lullaby*:

> With a lullaby on my lips anew —
> > Bang!
> I will drive the fear out of you —
> > Boom!
> Tuck your hand under your head, higher,
> Sleep tight, don't listen to the fire:
> > Fire!

Count Boris Fyodorovich Yurkevich had taken Klara Ivanovna out of a brothel. In Soviet Moscow he was a bookkeeper for an ordinary house management committee, in tsarist Warsaw he had been a special investigator.

The kitchen considered that "special" meant... Klara Ivanovna bristled:

"'Special' means 'criminal', if someone killed someone... How could you... Boris Fyodorovich!"

Boris Fyodorovich pronounced the word *bespasportny* (passportless) in the old, aristocratic manner — accent on the third syllable — and referred to "the October coup".

Like the Bernardessa, he too knew:

> Chizhik-Pyzhik where've you been?
> On Fontanka drinking gin.

On arriving home from work, he would have a small glass of vodka and a little piece of pickled herring with onion:

"For my appetite."

He didn't eat, but slowly partook, sending his silver spoon like a little scoop to his half-open mouth. He had — as did Alimpy — napkins in mother-of-pearl rings engraved with his name.

I always ate too quickly and burned my tongue. Mama edified:

"Look how beautifully Boris Fyodorovich eats."

In our apartment everyone knew exactly who ate what and how.

No one in our apartment was ever arrested because the first one to be arrested should have been Boris Fyodorovich — and he wasn't arrested because Klara Ivanovna was an i n f o r m e r.

She didn't work anywhere yet she received lengths of material and bought her food at various special stores. At some point those in a position to become fed up with her illiteracy became fed up and forced her to get a diploma. She was as nervous as a schoolgirl before her exams, and as exultant afterwards:

"I drew a question about, well, Finland — and I'd just read... in the paper..."

NKVD agents came to see her openly.

"We all hated Klar' 'Vanna," Mama recalled. "Once when no one was home I opened the door. He was alone, mug like a horse. Started askin' about the neighbors 'cross the hall. I said I didn't know anyone, had a child to look after. 'You must want Klar' 'Vanna,' I said. 'Yes,' he said, 'I'll come by again later.' "

Privileges the Yurkeviches may have had, but no money. Boris Fyodorovich earned next to nothing. Klara Ivanovna made a little at her sewing machine, but mostly she did small services: she did laundry, ran out to the store, tidied up. She would also stand in for the person whose turn it was to clean the corridor, the WC, the kitchen, the stove. God forbid you should refuse her services: she would turn the whole apartment against you. These feuds ended quickly though — just as soon as a new coalition had formed against a new ingrate.

When she went in town, Mama left me perforce with "Kayanna".

She would sit me on her double bed, and I would pour different colored buttons from one jar into another and back again. She was always impressed:

"And again you di'n' eat a single one!"

I liked to sew, to sew pieces of paper together:

"Needle the thread an' make a clot at th' end!"

Kayanna would thread the needle for me.

Sometimes she would lie down on the bed and I would burrow in under her chemise.

Klara Ivanovna had a rubber plant. Another rubber plant belonged to the Bernardessa. Klara Ivanovna owned the apartment's only dog — always a black and white Pomeranian, always named Tobik or Tobka, my best friend in Moscow. Before the war, and after the war, a birdcage hung in Klara Ivanovna's window — always a goldfinch with its songs and hempseed. Of all the people in our apartment, she was the only one who fed the pigeons out the kitchen window. Mama never once let me have a plant or an animal.

From Klara Ivanovna's window I could also make out the transparent — because of the columns — turret on top of Metropolitan Philipp's rotunda. In 1942, after reading "Secret Agent School" in *Young Pioneer* magazine, I began estimating distances by eye — everything turned out to be ridiculously far away. The transparent turret existed, I eventually saw it close up, but not from Klara Ivanovna's window.

Boris Fyodorovich addressed me in crisp, adult tones — like a clerk talking to a regular client. He r e c o m m e n d e d that I see the movie *If There's War Tomorrow*. He appointed me apartment head with a salary of 3 kopecks per six-day week. I said I'd rather be paid in bills.

One of Boris Fyodorovich's jokes: "A silly young lady is being taught social etiquette. 'First talk about the weather, then move on to music and, finally, say something pointed.' So she did:

> 'Oh, what marvelous weather!
> I've studied music forever...
> Knife!' "

Count Boris Fyodorovich lived the life of a mediocre bookkeeper, but sometimes he remembered who he was, took classics out of the Griboyedov Library, and gave dry reports to Aleksei Semyonovich in the kitchen:

"Zhukovsky has some pearls — as good as Pushkin."

When we annexed Latvia in 1940, Klara Ivanovna sang me a Latvian song she knew but drew the line at searching for her Latvian relatives. She had enough to do being an informer.

Nota bene: in the fall of '41 some of the neighbors asked Klara Ivanovna to put in a good word for them when the Germans came.

In hungry times, Klara Ivanovna and Boris Fyodorovich hid food from each other, hunted it down and ate it up. Having locked their door, the sinewy Latvian would flog the frail count and wail for the whole apartment to hear:

"He beats me, he beats me!"

Aleksei Semyonovich Litvinenko and Ekaterina Dmitrievna Matveyenko — Kursk natives descended from Ukrainians sent there under Catherine the Great — upheld the honor of their nation and spoke Russian with a deliberate drawl. The kitchen was incensed by the late-night telephone conversations of these outlanders: not because of the hour but because they were in Ukrainian. The kitchen insisted that no such language existed.

The kitchen resented the outlander-husband's habit of shaving twice a day, morning and evening...

His accented telephone conversations with colleagues and fellow-tribesmen grated.

"It's a question of different phonemes!" he countered. ("Phoneme," the kitchen repeated with distaste.)

Astonishingly, there were no scenes because of the telephone, even when they talked for hours, even when they talked on the long distance line — loudly, after midnight. The gas meter in the kitchen was quite another matter: next to it hung a copybook and a pencil stub on a string. The house wives calculated by some mysterious means how much gas they had used and wrote it down. Tonka was constantly suspected of cheating. Abuse — to the point of hoarseness — was hurled, however, not necessarily because of her, more likely it was simply that the time had come.

Klara Ivanovna was constantly washing, scraping, scrubbing — yet her own quarters were never clean. Ekaterina Dmitrievna spent long hours at the theater — yet the Litvinenkos' little room was always spotless. There wasn't even any dust, though the walls were crammed with books. From behind the glass door of a bookcase peered Hegel, resembling either a collie or a borzoi. Aleksei Semyonovich knew and valued philosophy no later than Kant/Hegel. Perhaps it was from this knowledge that his habitually threatening arrogance derived.

When her husband went off to the institute, Ekaterina Dmitrievna sat down at the upright piano and practiced her contralto vocalizations:

"aa aa aa aa, oo oo oo oo, ee ee ee ee..."

On the piano, on a starched tea towel, lay the music to the waltz *Over the Waves* with a couple in a rowboat, to *Sleep, Battling Eagles* with a war monument, and to Vertinsky's *Cadets* — Mama said to Ekaterina Dmitrievna that those cadets were the ones who defended the Kremlin in 1917:

"We all of us ran out to look at the dead, case there was someone we knew..."

Sometimes Ekaterina Dmitrievna sang:

> Weapons gleaming in the sun,
> As dashing trumpeters played...

She remembered, "When the White cavalry rode into Kursk..."
She liked to tell the story of how at one rehearsal of *La Belle Hélène*,
Nemirovich couldn't resist and stroked Kemarskaya's soft shoulders.
How Zoya Kosmodemyanskaya's mother came to see them:

"She gave a talk. She might at least have shed a tear or two.
She was her mother, after all."

She brought news from the theater:

"An escalator collapsed in the Metro, absolute meat-grinder..."

Once she gave us two free passes, not to the opera, where she
sang in the chorus ("She stands off to one side and just mouths the
words," the kitchen said), but to a Ukrainian ballet, *Christmas Eve*.
I went with Granny. During intermission I climbed out of our box
into the orchestra circle and back again. All in all I had such a good
time that instead of saying thank you I asked:

"Who gets to go for free every day?"

Ekaterina Dmitrievna thought for a moment:

"The fireman."

Now my dream was to become a fireman in a theater.
Sometime later Granny described the horrible condition of a burned
fireman brought into Sklifosovsky Hospital: t o o b a d, h e w a s
s o y o u n g...

Ekaterina Dmitrievna, seeing my love for beautiful things,
told me about the treasures kept by the man in charge of props.

Nemirovich's theater staged Ivan Derzhinsky's productions
of *Quiet Flows the Don* and *Virgin Soil Upturned*. In the kitchen
Ekaterina Dmitrievna acted out the scene where Grigory hides in a
haystack while Cossacks search for him and jab the haystack with
their sabers. She sang one role:

> Doomsday is at hand, one brother fights another,
> Everything is at odds, the Antichrist does hover...

then the other role, a recitative:

> Good children, they will build life anew,
> Genuine people there will be, genuine...

Presumably it was because of Ekaterina Dmitrievna and those operas that the kitchen went on debating year after year:

"Sholokhov didn't write *Quiet Flows the Don* himself..."

There were no objections, everyone wanted Sholokhov not to have written it himself, but who wanted to quash entertaining bits of gossip?

In her husband's absence Ekaterina Dmitrievna would invite me to look at their French books:

"Are your hands clean?"

"Yes, I just ate some bread."

"Go into the kitchen and wash them with soap!"

I imagined that it was the bread she distrusted: she always singed loaves from the store over a gas flame:

"The woman behind the counter wipes her runny nose with her hand, then hands you your bread."

In her room she showed me huge tomes the size of encyclopedias, and told me that the most beautiful cities on earth were not Paris and Leningrad but Buenos Aires and Rio de Janeiro.

Once she changed her clothes in front of me and I saw her enormous bosoms. Stunned, I asked what they were.

"Those are my two hearts, I can't be killed," she said, and jinxed herself.

While away on tour on the Volga she fell off a ship ladder and broke her skull.

Aleksei Semyonovich flew her body to Kursk — in an expensive zinc coffin of which the kitchen disapproved.

A few years later he married a lady by the not accidental name of Bromley.

The year before the war broke out, Aleksei Semyonovich gave me a scare. He came to Papa to ask for advice in filling out a form. I peeked over his shoulder and after the *Party Membership* question saw the letters b/p. I knew that b stood for *byvshii* (formerly priviledged classes) and I knew what happened to people like that. It was some time before Papa explained to me that b/p stood for *bespartiiny* (non-Party).

Aleksei Semyonovich ignored me. Only once, when I was five, he sat me on his writing desk, gave me the box from a bottle of *Red Poppy* perfume, and took a phenomenal snapshot.

And during the bombing of London he showed me the bottom half of a picture in the *Daily Worker*: tubes, tubes, tubes, all running parallel to one another.

"Guess what that is!"

I guessed, but didn't say out of politeness. He handed me the photograph of an enormous fire with parallel firemen and hoses.

Mama asked Aleksei Semyonovich if he had a copy of *Huckleberry Finn*.

"Yes, in Ukrainian," he refused her.

Over the years I was increasingly — if reluctantly — obliged to go to him to ask about a stamp or a coin or a medal. Gradually his heart softened.

In '47 I consulted him about what kind of radio to buy. He was pleased when Papa and I came home from the second-hand store with a *Telefunken*. He knew all there was to know: before the war he had put out a six-language dictionary of radio engineering and procured a magnificent 6-N-1, confiscated in '41 when all radios were confiscated. On the 6-N-1 before the war everything was as clear as Moscow — a little louder, a little softer. When I heard foreign speech on the radio it always sounded to me like people swearing.

After the war Aleksei Semyonovich bought one of the very first VEFs ever produced, with a round dial. He made me see that I must listen so as to pick up English more quickly. He loaned me a book for a couple of weeks about American Boy Scouts.

He taught me photography. He explained that the best camera was an FED — a prewar one, from something to something thousand. He cautioned against pictures of sparkling, frost-covered trees: simply common. He criticized my first shots and showed me his own, superb ones.

In winter he went skiing in the country, in summer he went on long walking expeditions. He had been to the Field of Kulikovo and photographed the site's Suvorov-like custodian:

"An extraordinary man!"

From near Fet's estate he had returned with positively Fetian landscapes, intensified so as to look old, and a darkened brick with a round stamp: SHENSHIN. To his chagrin, the old men he had met there remembered the landowner but knew nothing of the poet.

Aleksei Semyonovich introduced me to Ukrainian poetry. Early Tychina, the vanished Dmitro Zagul, pre-revolutionary Rylsky and, in deference to my Futurism, Mikhail Semenko — a two-volume anthology (1930) minus the binding, but with the portraits.

I was fond of Velimir Khlebnikov. Aleksei Semyonovich showed me a booklet by a Petrozavodsk teacher named Martynov who maintained that human speech consisted of "senspirations".

"Senspirations. Just think of it, in the 1890s!.."

In the early '20s Aleksei Semyonovich had studied at Bryusov's institute and recalled that the Symbolist poet saw each and every student as an enemy and a rival.

Aleksei Semyonovich insisted that I read the classics the way I would contemporary writers — critically and partially:

"Do you realize that Pushkin's *the day's light has gone out* is an adaptation from Byron? Have you noticed that *docile sail, sing out, sing out* is absurd? If a sail is full of wind, it can't sing out, it makes no noise."

Aleksei Semyonovich gave me a lesson in political literacy:

"Marxism occupies the same place in the system of philosophy as your shoes do in the system of musical instruments."

I brought Aleksei Semyonovich samples of my writing. He pompously pointed out the incongruities, upbraided me for my artificial tone, and shamed me for my sloppy Russian:

"You should listen to how your mother talks!"

He would often fly into the kitchen, straight from his writing desk, and demand that Mama read — without thinking about it — a word written on a slip of paper. By way of thanks he once told an American joke:

"In New York one day a Jew named Rabinowitz changes his name to Kirkpatrick. A few days later he changes his name again — to MacMagon. 'Rabinowitz, why'd you do that?' 'Because people will ask me, Mr. MacMagon what was your name before?' And I'll say, 'Kirkpatrick.' "

After the notorious 1948 session of the Academy of Agricultural Sciences, Aleksei Semyonovich buttonholed Papa and whispered in his ear:

"I can't understand it, Lysenko — it's Lamarckism!"

Stalin's *Marxism and Linguistics* had deprived him of a well-deserved professorship:

"We were always told to base ourselves on Marr. Now that basis has been taken away from us, and we've been given nothing in exchange..."

Aleksei Semyonovich came to Papa for advice on practical, work and everyday matters, and always declared grandly:

"I so admire Yakov Artemevich! The clarity of his outlook on life is worthy of wonder."

FATHER

If she hadn't been pregnant with me, Mama would hardly have married Father. To the end of her days Granny thought it a *mesalliance*. In the Trubnikovs' grand house she had seen the elegant life and dreamed that her daughters, when they became young ladies, would never work — which is exactly what happened, only God forbid how.

Granny sang:

> He carted cabbage on his mother-in-law's back,
> Saddled up his wife with the horse's tack:
> Get a move on, Granny, run for your life!
> Whoa! Hold on there, my young wife!

In my presence she often said: "The swine! Took a wife as if he'd bought a cow."

Father was: A country bumpkin. Insensitive. Indiscriminate. Inattentive. Inconsiderate. And where did he work? At the Timiryazev Agricultural Academy:

> No one wears fancy spurs there,
> Or fires from a gun,
> Or fires from a gun.
> The students all milk cows there.
> And make hay in the sun,
> And make hay in the sun — Tra-la-la!

On the other hand, what else could Mama do? The apartment on Bolshaya Ekaterininskaya had been turned into a communal apartment, leaving her family with just two — communicating — rooms: Granny and Grandfather shared one, Mama and Vera the other.

"I could never invite anyone in. If someone came by, Vera would stretch out on her bed, face the wall and refuse to leave. Just to spite me. Yakov's room was small, but his own."

It was small, but it had all the modern conveniences: central heating, gas, a bath, later a telephone, and — best of all — it was around the corner from Bolshaya Ekaterininskaya, from Granny's.

When Mama moved to Kapelsky Lane, Granny and Grandfather lay awake the whole night: Father was s i m p l e but s e c r e t i v e — who could make him out? Could be a communizer, could be o n e   o f   t h e m.

Life on Kapelsky went badly from the start: Father's mother, Ksenia Kirillovna, appeared suddenly from the country.

"Sat on top of us for two weeks. 'S if she didn't know any better, damned fool. Can't tell you how sick of her I got. Kept givin' me dirty looks: he's taken a young lady. And he was no help: should've told her. She could've gone to Avdotia and Ivan's: he was her son too. And he had two rooms. In summer, in Udelnaya, they were happy to have her so long as she looked after their little boy Seryozha. But in winter, in Moscow, not for all the tea in China!"

Mama was also considered a young lady in Udelnaya. Father's brother Ivan, an agronomist, was a rustic like his wife Avdotia, out of a teachers' training college. They both loved the earth and would dig in the garden till dark. Mama was a city girl, she didn't worship the earth: she had neither the desire nor the need.

Before Mama came along, they had lived in one half of the Udelnaya dacha and rented out the other. Mama objected:

"Absolutely not! You can hear everythin' through the wall, you can practically see everythin'!"

Sullen Ivan stayed out of it, as was his wont, while wicked Avdotia said for everyone to hear:

"Know where Yakov picked her up? On Tsvetnoi Boulevard."

"How do you know?"

"Everyone knows but you, you fool."

Mama complained to Father. Relations between the brothers became strained.

Whether that was the way it was or not, I don't know.

In this society, on a half-empty plot barely enclosed by poles, Mama stuck it out with me from May until October or November. The stray cows frightened her, still more the gypsies.

Through the wall, Seryozha could be heard asking Ksenia Kirillovna:

"Gram, oh, Gram, want me to walk to the station bare?"

Mama got along poorly with the neighboring dachas, the Tikhonovs and the Bogoslovskys: to their faces she fawned, but behind their backs she turned up her nose. She never invited friends from Moscow. To make life easier, she let Matyonna, my nanny, come out. Granny appeared in any weather: sink or swim. She always brought us something delicious and expensive: caviar, salmon, sturgeon, ham — if only a hundred grams.

Father was faulted for never having brought Mama anything from the Foreign Trade Store when she was in the maternity hospital with me. The times were such that when Granny brought Mama an orange, the ward turned on her:

"Bourgeois..."

Father spent vacations pottering in the garden. Otherwise, he came out every Saturday for the night. He brought groats, sugar: the food in Udelnaya, in the village commissary, was marked up.

Father did most of the marketing — and any other errands. Mama was too lazy. She reasoned:

"It's not me who earns the money..."

Father didn't earn much, but still he earned more than Grandfather and Granny put together.

At loose ends one day, Mama left me with Matyonna and skipped off to Moscow, to Kapelsky Lane.

"I walked in the door and there he was, cheeks sleek, eatin' a frankfurter, when all I had in Udelnaya was cold kvass soup..."

A difference in upbringing: Father could polish off a pan of fried potatoes, Mama was repelled:

"How revoltin'! Sight of those potatoes makes me sick!"

Father raised his eyebrows in surprise: the second and most terrible famine had only just ended.

He didn't care for dainties, delicacies, seasonings and *sentimental slop*: food should be filling, fattening and full of vitamins; he was an associate professor in the alimentation department.

As a special treat — on Sundays for tea — he would toast bread.

Canned foods were essential: canned meat could occasionally be had even in Udelnaya. Sprats were a luxury: we bought them once or twice before the war. Ekaterina Dmitrievna once gave me a teaspoonful of condensed milk to try. Bowled me over.

The bologna Father bought twice a month on paydays — two hundred grams sliced paper-thin — sent me into raptures. Sometimes Father would put a slice of cheese on top of his bologna, making a d o u b l e - d e c k e r sandwich, like the double-decker trolleybus on First Meshchanskaya Street.

In summer we never bought watermelons, muskmelons, peaches or apricots: he thought our own fruit and berries sufficed.

But one winter, when oranges appeared for the first time in years — from Spain — Father brought home a whole basketful (this was before string-bags); he stood in line for them to boot.

Mama was considered a good cook. When I first heard the expression "national dish", I decided that Russia's national dishes must be potato soup with sour cream, and cutlets with kasha or mashed potatoes.

That is exactly what Father liked; in the evening, after work, he always asked for a second helping. I liked those things too. I was never given fried meat: too tough to chew anyway. Pickled herring, for some reason, seemed to me an indecent food — perhaps because of the smell it left on the forks and knives. Father ate no fish of any kind: bones.

Father was setting money aside. He wanted to swap our one room for two rooms, making up the difference in cash. Mama agreed in principle, but rejected every offer: she was afraid to live even a step further from Granny.

Father grumbled that newcomers to Moscow were given separate apartments, whereas native Muscovites...

I had never seen a separate apartment — the Trubnikovs' stunned me, like a miracle of nature. As a rule, people did not live in their own apartments, but occupied floor-space — some more, some less — in communal ones. Our existence, the three of us, in one 13-square-meter room with two enormous windows and a canted corner did not strike me as abnormal.

How I loved Mama! In Udelnaya my first morning impulse was towards her (her trestle bed was in Papa's room, but she slept on another — in my room). The most beautiful, the most familiar, the most comforting of all. She understood me better than anyone else.

Father meanwhile...

Father was at the academy from morning till night. Granny/

Mama appropriated and spoiled me. Seeing the result, Father sighed:

"Sloth was born before you were."

He was often defeated even before he'd begun to object, and he washed his hands of me:

"Your child, you bring him up."

For every one word of Papa's, Mama came back at him with ten.

She exasperated him:

"Let me get a word in!" When she kept him from his work, he would snap: "Go back in your stall!"

He was insultingly s i m p l e, s t r a p p i n g and s t r o n g a s a n o x, in all the years before the war he was ill only once — with malaria, silently and uninterestingly.

Mama was constantly i n d i s p o s e d, she loved to tell Granny and me just how and where it had come over her, about the stitches, the spasms, the pit-a-pats. I considered indisposition a matter of good form and, copying Mama, complained of real and imaginary pains. Father didn't like it:

"The evening sacrifice."

For his degree requirements, Father managed — just barely — to master Halperin's English textbook; on forms he wrote: *reading knowledge of English*. Mama entered into my fascination with France and taught me a bit of French and German.

Father knew his Nekrasov. Mama preferred Balmont and Severyanin. She said they were "aesthetes". In a varnished keepsake album she had from her school days, I read:

> Please forgive this silly scrawl:
> I'm banging my head against the wall

> Then because of the terrible pain,
> You'll think of me again and again.

and at the very bottom of the last bound page was the apothegm quoted by Pushkin:

> I entered a verse of my own in the little album, in large letters:

> O'er dark blue taigan floes
> An ancient fisherman goes.
> 21/III — 1941

This was undoubtedly the radio's influence. (I also remembered Borya's and my riverside rambles:

> A raft drifts by,
> Grass waist-high,
> And a dead dragon-fly.)

In our family Father was the only one who liked Russian songs — only not sung by the Aleksandrov Military Choir. Mama dismissed everything Russian as folksey. On the radio she listened to Massenet's *Elegy*— Chaliapin's long-drawn-out m-m-m — and to *Aria with Bells* sung by Barsova, the coloratura. She didn't take sides in the Kozlovsky-Lemeshev feud. She agreed that Kozlovsky had a beautiful way of drawing out his *l-l-love* and possessed the stronger voice, but admitted that Lemeshev's had a *pleasant timbre*. She often recalled Sobinov and how Chaliapin, furious with Shuisky in *Boris Godunov*, had grabbed him by the beard — and that beard was only glued on...

She and Father even had different words for things. When we harvested a strawberry the size of my fist, Mama: "Humdinger!"

Father: "Maybe a hundred grams..."

Father joked:

> Oh me, oh dear,
> Said Mr. Greer,
> My last pair of pants,
> And they're gone in the rear.

I didn't think it was funny.

He wrung his hands: "If for worshipping God it's not, it's for covering your chamber pot."

I couldn't understand what he meant.

When he found a bird dropping on his shoulder: "It left me its card." I fidgeted.

He ironized: "Give me a little one of those the size of a cow's nose." I winced.

When he disapproved of someone: "Jackass. Joe Schmo." I could see by Granny/Mama's faces that they used those same words about Father.

They blamed him for the whole eparchy: for himself, for Ivan and Avdotia, for Granny Ksenia:

"Only one she cares about is Seryozha, her little Seryozha. There's no one here to leave Andrei with..."

Which must mean that Matyonna was no longer my nanny.

I did occasionally stay with Granny Ksenia. I looked into her left, unseeing eye and listened to her dreary tales of rustic life. Once she acted out an epic poem for me:

> ...Count Paskevich
> Was going on the march,
> And on the march he did go,
> His regiments behind him,
> The dust swirling behind him.

I sided with Balmont and Massenet, I hadn't grown to love the earth, I hadn't grown to love Granny Ksenia, and for Father I had coined the hurtful nickname "Stepfather". After reading *The Prince and the Pauper*, I began raving about my noble birth.

A person has missed something important in the correlation between the possible and the impossible if, as a child, he has never suspected his parents of not being his real parents.

Mine were the very realest of parents.

Around 1950, behind the couch, I found boxes of splendid old glass negatives — larger than postcards — and printed them.

A photograph of the Sergeev family. Circa 1910. In the village of Zhukovka.

In front of a log hut with big, tall — un-rustic — windows with carved platbands, eight people are seated not on the usual mound of carried earth, but on a bench running the length of the wall.

The gaunt patriarch is wearing a Cossack coat, a scraggly beard, and a look of Nekrasovian suffering.

His wife, Granny Ksenia, clad in a dark, flowered scarf and a dark, floor-length skirt, is severe-looking and self-important enough for two.

Her slightly more inventive daughter-in-law is holding a sobbing grandchild in a cap and warm clothes — he has the smallpox.

A wooden horse with a tail, but no head.

The eldest son Pavel has the capable look of a workingman; he's wearing a blouse with a collar that fastens at the side and a jacket — and a small moustache for respectability.

Kirill, a student, is in a peaked cap, looking straight at the camera and sniggering.

Ivan, to my complete surprise, has a bright, smiling face beneath his own peaked cap. He, too, is a student.

Yakov — Father — is slightly out of focus: he's the one taking the photograph, he has just wound up the shutter and sat down to one side: a gentleman in a flat hat, three-piece suit and rounded stand-up collar, legs crossed, pants creased.

A ninth person — white against the white wall — has the look of a convalescent. A tenth is in front of everyone else astride another wooden horse, also in a peaked cap. One of them is Fyodor, the other is Pavel's first son, I don't know his name.

Of course, they had all smartened themselves up for the photograph. Everyone is wearing tie shoes and everyone — except the patriarch and his wife — has his eye on the city.

The only thing older than this photograph is a small bronze triptych of St. Nicholas the Miracle-worker; my great grandfather, the father of the patriarch in the photograph, wore it at Sevastopol, during the Crimean War.

This is how they lived: they rented their landlady's cows for the winter, they had their own hay and, with the manure, the fields produced what they should. There was never any drinking.

After the local three-year school, the teacher sent the brightest — including my father — to Shchapovo.

Studio portrait by I.D. Danilov. Moscow, Myasnitskye Vorota, Kabanov house, opposite telegraph office. Negatives in storage. In my father's hand: *18/XII — 1905*, in other words he's sixteen. He's wearing his weekday coat, his hair is combed, his forehead well proportioned and modeled, his face thoughtful — the face of a student, an intellectual of humble, but not apparently peasant, origin.

In a group shot of the Shchapovo school's first graduating class, all twenty students look on the plain side, some of them rather coarse, and Father does not stand out. His ability to blend in would prove useful later on.

Russian State Seal. Ornate type:
CERTIFICATE No. 628

This certificate has been issued by the Pedagogic Council of the Shchapovo Crown Agricultural School first class, in accordance with Art. 35 of the school rules, over the proper signature and seal affixed, to Sergeev, Yakov Artemevich, a student of said school, which he entered in 1903, completing the full course of studies in 1907 and earning the following marks on his final examinations:

1) General Subjects:

Religion — good 4.

Russian — good 4.

Arithmetic — very good 4 1/2.

Geometry — very good 4 1/2.

Land Surveying — good 4.

Drawing — good 4.

Geography — very good 4 1/2.

Russian history — good 4.

Physics — good 4.

Chemistry — good 4.

Botany — very good 4 1/2.

Zoology — excellent 5.

2) Special Subjects:

Agriculture — excellent 5.

Forestry — did not study.

Animal Husbandry — excellent 5.

Horticulture and Gardening — excellent 5.

Agricultural Economics and Bookkeeping — excellent 5.

Jurisprudence — excellent 5.

    3) Apprenticeships:

Joinery — studied.

Locksmithing and Blacksmithing — studied.

    4) Practical Work:

Agriculture — excellent 5.

Animal Husbandry — excellent 5.

Horticulture and Gardening — excellent 5.

While attending the school his, Sergeev's, behavior was excellent.

In accordance with Art. 37 of the school rules he, Sergeev, enjoys a second-class exemption from military duty.

From documents submitted by Sergeev, it is clear that he was born on 16 October 1889, that he is of peasant origin and of the Orthodox confession.

Village of Aleksandrovo, Moscow Province, Podolsk Uyezd, August the 22nd, 1907.

            School director — (signature).

            Teachers — (signatures).

            Council Secretary — (signature).

Stamp with the Moscow seal.

I cite documents: they, too, are photographs from a time gone by. I cite dates: too many coincide with notorious dates from the time in which my father lived, a time to which he was in part a witness, but never a party.

For a start: in 1889 Hitler was born and the Eiffel Tower built. That same year Anna Akhmatova was born. My father would have been happy never to have heard of them his whole life.

        AGRICULTURAL ASSOCIATION
        PODOLSK UYEZD, MOSCOW PROV.
        JANUARY the 28th, 1914. No. 319.

CERTIFICATE

This is issued to Yakov Sergeev, peasant of Zhukovka Village, Podcherkov Volost, Dmitrov Uyezd, Moscow Province, in witness of the fact that he, upon finishing Shchapovo Crown Agricultural School 1st class on 22 August 1907, did assume the post of manager of the Senkin estate, then in the usufruct of the Podolsk Agricultural Association, in which post he remained until 22 October 1911. Sergeev acquitted himself of his duties in an entirely conscientious and careful manner, the estate farm during Sergeev's stewardship was in entirely satisfactory condition. Sergeev left his office at the Senkin estate by reason of his enlistment for military duty.

> Chairman of the Association — (signature).
> Secretary — (signature).
> Stamp with double-headed eagle.

In Soviet times, this certificate would have been called a character reference and would have borne no relation to reality. But in those days words still retained their meaning. *Entirely conscientious and entirely satisfactory* meant entirely conscientious and entirely satisfactory. *Military duty* was military duty.

Father began managing the estate — the pedigree breeding of cattle and pigs — when he wasn't yet eighteen. He strode about the place as master — with a steel *Mauser* watch on a chain (until quite recently it was accurate to the minute). According to the custom then, Father was entitled, apart from his salary, to a free apartment and whatever the farm he oversaw produced.

"Everything was simpler then, people lived more openly and weren't afraid. They would look in on you if they saw a light in the window. In the evening I'd order the droshky and drive seven versts to a neighbor's. What did we do? Drank tea, played cards. One winter I read all of Chekhov. And Vlas Doroshevich's *Sakhalin*.

At Shchapovo we got up an amateur production of *The Marriage*: I played the bride..."

In that era of aviation pioneers Bleriot and Utochkin, boys would troop into Moscow and attract jostling crowds in any street:

"Look! There he is! No, no! Not there! A little to the left... Above that pipe. Now he's lower down, lower still. Just above that green roof. Right by the eaves. In the corner! Don't you see him? There he is! He's right there!" The instigators would slip away unnoticed. Back then this was considered an art in a most worldly sense.

Father never smoked or drank. He sought out his intellectual equals — his friend Kachkin — or betters, those he could learn from: a descendant of Gogol-Yanovsky; Mendeleev's son, an agronomist, he died at twenty-six — of botulism. After that Father was always wary of canned food. A present survived: *Mendeleev's mug* — large and thick to keep from breaking, it had been used on shipboard. Mendeleev himself was supposed to have drunk from it.

Father's brother Pavel, the eldest son, could not be conscripted; the first to enlist was Yakov. Because of his education, he was allowed to stay where he was as an Army volunteer. Why for so long is unclear. His military duty wasn't hard, he had time and savings to spare. This is when he took up photography.

Scene. Three soldiers on the porch of a two-story house. A sign over the door reads: ADMINISTRATION OF THE PODOLSK MILITARY COMMANDER, and a little plaque: HOUSE No. 94 CITY OF PODOLSK. A letterbox with an eagle and an envelope drawn on it, and over it: RECEPTION OF POSTAL DISPATCHES TAKES PLACE AT 12:30 IN THE AFTERNOON AND AT 8:00 IN THE EVENING.

Self-portrait on an iron cot. Reclining, cheek cupped in palm, elbow deep in two white pillows; a newspaper in his left hand. An oval name-plate on an iron bar at the head of the bed reads: No. 5, COP. STU. YAKOV SERGEEV 1912.

Five soldiers under a brittle willow.

Five soldiers in a quarry.

Eight soldiers outside a crown office.

A string orchestra. Father with a balalaika. The faces in these photographs are handsome and homely, plainer and more refined — but all are composed and comely.

Gymnastics pyramids made up of dozens of soldiers. Officers in the bottom. The little one with the paunch and the pince-nez is the Podolsk military commander. Unlike the other officers, he is wearing gaiters instead of boots, and on his full-dress uniform there isn't a single decoration or medal, only a regimental badge. The soldiers in the pyramids look dashing, while the officers under them look pleased and proud.

The military commander with his wife and daughter — already past her prime and languishing — by the samovar. Here, too, he is wearing his peaked cap: lest the photograph reveal his practice of painting his bald spot.

Father never took pictures of himself without his moustache. Once he shaved it off — just to see. The sergeant major upbraided him publicly:

"You old Polish broad!"

An omission: there isn't one shot of Kononenko, Podolsk's own good soldier Svejk. A piece of lore: the sergeant major asks:

"Kononenko, who is our sovereign emperor?"

"Sovereign emperor... Maria Fyodorovna!"

"For whom are we ready to lay down our life?"

"Lay down our life... For Maria Fyodorovna!"

"Who is our enemy, external and internal?"

"External and internal... Maria Fyodorovna!"

In another photograph the pyramid has thinned out and looks gloomy against a background of pitted brick and a rickety arcade:

A freakishly tall circus acrobat cum militiaman with a cross on his cartouche and a rifle propped against his leg — it comes up only to his waist. Officers are having their photograph taken next to him. The war is on.

Father had somehow been assigned to a Siberian marching regiment doomed to perish in the Carpathian Mountains. At the last minute, the Podolsk military commander recalled him. Just before boarding the train:

"Sergeev, you're staying with me. But you'll lose your rank of volunteer. Understood?"

Of course, understood. Why did the commander save him? Was Father an irreplaceable copyist? A personal favorite? Had someone put in a good word? Was he a potential husband for a daughter?

This was to be the pattern throughout Father's life: someone always saved him.

The last soldier picture. A little garden, a fence. Father is reclining in lordly fashion beside a flowerbed in a white soldier's tunic. His shoulder straps show two badges of rank. The non-commissioned officer's rank would soon have to be concealed.

Father didn't care about politics, but in the summer of 1917 — again because of being educated — he headed up a minor non-Party council. This too had to be concealed from the Soviet regime.

In November his brother Ivan brought two boys out from Moscow:

"Cadets from the Kremlin."

Being his own boss, Father issued them documents.

In the Constituent Assembly elections, he voted for the People's Socialists — they were almost Socialist Revolutionaries, only against terror, like the Constitutional Democrats.

"In Podolsk we had one landowner. They burned his manor to the ground. He was left with his house in Podolsk and one thousand silver rubles for the whole family. He said to the yard-keeper: 'Such hard times. I'm afraid to hide the money in the house. Vassily, you go and bury it in the garden.' Couldn't do it himself! When he thought of it again, the money was gone. And that Vassily was devoted to him. He must have told someone, must have bragged..."

After the *Revolushit*, Father realized that the new regime liked documents: he began amassing them, barricading himself in with them, and making notarized copies against the future.

CERTIFICATE No. 930

Soldier Yakov Artemevich Sergeev of the Podolsk Uyezd Military Commander's Administration, conscripted in 1911, descended from citizens in the village of Zhukovka, Podcherkov volost, Dmitrov uyezd, Moscow prov., in compliance with order No. 158, 1918, issued to the Moscow Military Command Forces, is discharged from service altogether, witness the signature and official seal affixed.

23 February 1918, City of Podolsk, Mosc. Prov. Podolsk Uyezd Military Commander; Member of the Soviet of Workers', Soldiers' and Peasants' Deputies — Kachkin.

Secretary — (signature).

The seal (with the double-headed eagle but without the

crowns), the pre-revolutionary spellings in the text, the content and the language all come from the Provisional Government. *Nota bene*: "citizens in the village of Zhukovka" instead of *peasants*. The paper — a sheet torn out of a copybook and then in half — comes from Bolshevism.

Father left the military office without bothering to lock the safe full of gilded Provisional Government military decorations, he escaped the Civil War.

How did he manage it? Did Kachkin, his friend from the Senkin estate, help him? Did the pattern? Either way, Father's favorite saying — with a twist — was borne out:

Don't boast upon riding out to battle, boast upon returning.

From Father's curriculum vitae, dated 1948:

> From 19 February 1918 until 1 March 1919, I worked as secretary of the Podolsk District Land Department and then as manager of Dubrovitsy State Farm in the Podolsk district, which belonged at the time to the Moscow District Land Department. From 1 March until 15 December 1919, I attended courses at Timiryazev Agricultural Academy.

This, in essence, is a translation from Leninese to Stalinese. The odious date of his demobilization (23 February 1918) has been amended to a neutral one. The Uyezd Land Department has turned into the District Land Department, and the Peter the Great Agricultural Academy into Timiryazev. Only Dubrovitsy remained:

"The church in Dubrovitsy was marvelous... historic."

And an intensified violet photograph of Dubrovitsy baroque.

An ancient sheet of lined paper; a rubber stamp in one corner; and the following in longhand:

People's Commissariat of Agriculture

Department of Animal Husbandry

Instructors' Courses in Animal Husbandry and Dairy Farming

October the 18th, 1919 No. 200

Moscow, Agric. Acad.

CERTIFICATE

On the basis of the Moscow Defense Committee's resolution concerning the registration of the non-working population published in No. 211 of the *All-Russian Central Executive Committee News*, 23 September 1919, this certificate is issued by the Instructors' Courses in Animal Husbandry and Dairy Farming to comrade Sergeev, Yakov Artemevich, born in 1889, in that he is enrolled in the aforementioned courses in the Animal Husbandry Department of the People's Commissariat of Agriculture, witness the signature and seal affixed.

Acting Director — (signature)

Secretary — (signature)

Stamp with the RSFSR seal

On the back are official entries referring to parcels sent to Moscow and postmarked USOLYE, SIMBIRSK Region.

17/III to I.A. Sergeev, Podolsk, Mosc. 17 dry lbs.

28/IV to A.K. Oshtukov for K.K. Sergeeva, Dmitrov, Mosc. 19 dry lbs.

12 May to Sergeev, F.A., 13 dry lbs.

4 June to A.S. Panova 20 dry lbs.

25/VI — '20 to K. Kir. Sergeeva 19 dry lbs.

16/Jul 1920 to Kachkin — 15 dry lbs.

31/VIII — '20 to Yakovlev, Moscow, 19 dry lbs.

I.A. and F.A. Sergeev were Father's brothers.

K.K. Sergeeva was his mother.

Kachkin was his friend.

A.S. Panova was ?

Yakovlev — Mitrofan Nikolaevich or Mitrosha, for short — was a former Shchapovo teacher, a Constituent Assembly deputy, evidently a Socialist Revolutionary, and practically a minister on the Samara Committee of Constituent Assembly Members. He wasn't shot thanks to the intervention of an acquaintance, Margarita Fofanova — the one who hid Lenin from the tsarist police, and for whom Lenin left a note the night of October 24 (1917):

"I've gone where you did not want me to go."

In Moscow, War Communism reigned. The authorities handed out steel cufflinks — official style — and arrested many Podolsk acquaintances. They had gotten together on their cadet corps anniversary and sung *God Save the Tsar*. Prince Volkonsky, they suspected, had informed.

Father lived for a time in the Solodovka, an enormous building, a first-class example of Viennese art nouveau, full of tiny rooms with all the conveniences for the poor. Built by a philanthropist, the merchant Solodovnikov, it adorned Second Meshchanskaya Street — a stone's throw from wooden, architectureless Bolshaya Ekaterininskaya.

Academy extension courses supplemented Father's income.

"Now I'll tell you how I speculated. In Shilov Uyezd, near Ryazan, during my practical work. There they gave us all milk and curds, they gave us cheese — Dutch cheese we made ourselves. The milk and curds we ate, but not the cheese. Once I took a wheel of cheese to Moscow. I sold the cheese — and with the proceeds bought myself a whole winter coat. You could see it was a good one: in 1930, I had it altered. The front turned out to be stuffed with eiderdown. I wore it right up until the war."

Yakovlev sent father away from hungry Moscow — again the pattern — to Usolye. Many Muscovites and Petersburgers escaped famine there at the Middle-Volga Agricultural College. For titled persons Yakovlev devised fantastic sinecures. Father actually worked — as a lecturer in the department of animal husbandry and as manager of the pedigree farm.

"This was at the Orlov-Davydov estate. We sent parcels to Moscow from Usolye. Someone informed on Mitrosha, said he was sending lots of food to Moscow. We were sitting behind a screen and heard the whole thing. At Mikhail Savelovich's, the volost elder's. The tsar, you know, wasn't guarded by police in Moscow, only by village elders. Hired in the provinces. When the tsar rode along the Garden Ring Road, elders linked arms on both sides to hold back the crowds..."

Father often recalled the merry life in Usolye, Mitrosha's amorous adventures, and their not knowing what would be more delicious — chicken in sour cream or apples in sweet cream.

Mama was always indignant:

"Havin' his apple baked in cream when all we had to eat was herrin'."

By the time famine set in on the Volga, Father had returned to Moscow. It's hard to imagine how he worked as a lecturer in the department of cattle-breeding and livestock alimentation at Moscow Zootechnical Institute while managing the institute's experimental-training farm *Rodniki* (*Chudakovo*) and studying at the same institute. Except that the rector there was Fofanova, and then Yakovlev.

To reconstruct: he rose before dawn, assigned chores, then went round the cattle-yard or drove out into the fields. Chudakovo, now Novaya Malakhovka, was across the Makedonka River from

Udelnaya. (In the late '20s, it had been the site of the Communist University for Workers of the East and t w o C h i n a m e n d r o w n e d.) The closest station was at least a verst off; Father must have been taken there in a cart. Then an hour or more on the train — the infrequent local steam-trains of the early '20s could hardly have been so under-subscribed as to allow a person to read in the cars. In those first years Father made his way to the institute — from Moscow's Kazan Station to Smolensky Boulevard — on foot. After the institute, it was back to Chudakovo and respons-ibilities there until dark: the cattle-yard, practical work with students, lectures for peasants. Before collectivization, educating farmers was considered good for the Revolution. The estate had to be closely watched to prevent pilfering, besides which the roof had to be repaired, the wallpaper replaced, the pond cleaned. To keep the place looking more or less as it had under its owner. From Father I heard that Chudakovo — like almost everything else in Russia — had belonged to Count Sheremetev.

The two-story manor house — with a garden and a pond and its own fresh produce — was rented out to good tenants. Celebrated tenants — the tragic actor brothers Adelheim — and hardly by chance: neighboring Malakhovka had a stylish, white, wooden summer theater where the best Maly and Korsh actors performed. Later I went there — to a shabby summer cinema that had been touched up with whatever came to hand.

> PERSONAL RECORD (form No. 4) dated 5/IV — '23
> In longhand across one corner of the paper cover:
> Residence permit issued by the Bykovo Volost Executive
> Committee 30/V 1924
> Chairman — (signature)

In the middle of the cover in bold type:

PASSPORT ISSUED 33.

Inside: Military category No. 53.

Name, patronymic, surname, date and place of birth, and then:

4. a) Military rank in the old army: private.

b) Position in the Red Army: none.

5. Military vocation: copyist.

6. Participated in which campaigns: none.

7. Wounded, shell-shocked, poisoned by gases: no.

8. General education (civilian): secondary.

9. Military education:

10. Athletic training:

11. Party affiliation: none.

12. Marital status: single.

13. Family members and number of dependents: 2; 1.

14. Principal profession: manager of pedigree stock farm

15. Other professions: none.

16. If a member of a trade union, state which one:

All-Russian Union of Farm and Timber Workers

A thick sheet of paper twice the size of an ordinary one. A dirty gold, almost funereal frame. Over the faded photograph of an old man in a cap and bow tie:

> The 18th of December 1924
> GRADUATING CLASS OF THE MOSCOW
> ZOOTECHNICAL INSTITUTE NAMED AFTER
> PROFESSOR P.N. KULESHOV
> CERTIFICATE (temporary)

This certificate is issued to citizen Sergeev, Yakov Artemevich, in that he was a student at the Moscow Zootechnical Institute, completed all the theoretical and practical courses in agronomic and zootechnical sciences, and passed the final examinations:

Physics	Prof.	S. I. Vavilov
Inorganic Chemistry	"	M. N. Popov
Organic Chemistry		
Mineralogy, Geology	"	N. Z. Milkovich
Botany	"	L. M. Krechetovich
Zoology	"	N. V. Bogoyavlensky
Political Economy	"	M. N. Nersesov
Agric. Geography and Statistics	"	E. D. Moshkov
Agric. Policy	"	M. M. Shulgin
Social Science	Inst.	M. E. Kosterin
Agronomic Chemistry	Prof.	Ya. P. Korolyov
Microbiology	"	N.Ya. Mikhin
Comparative Anatomy	"	V. A. Deinega
Anatomy of Animals and Histology	"	A. F. Klimov
Physiology of Animals	"	M. N. Shaternikov
Soil Science, Meadow Science	"	M. P. Grigoriev
General Farming	"	A. A. Bauer
Specialized Farming Meadow Cultivation	"	M. P. Grigoriev
Agric. Engineering	"	D. D. Artsybashev
Building Design	"	N. N. Bekhterev
Cultivation	"	N. A. Yurasov
Genetics	Inst.	A. S. Serebrovsky
Alimentation	Prof.	I. S. Popov
Technology of Milk	"	A. A. Popov
	Inst.	R. E. Gerlakh
Chemistry of Milk	"	G. S. Inikhov
Bacteriology of Milk	"	A. F. Voitkevich
Zoohygiene	"	N. V. Zelenin
Veterinary Science	Prof.	G. M. Andrievsky
Horse Breeding	"	P. N. Kuleshov

Cattle	"	E. F. Liskun
Pig Breeding	Inst.	M. N. Yakovlev
Sheep Breeding	Prof.	P. N. Kuleshov
Poultry Farming	"	V. P. Nikitin
Fattening of Farm Animals	Inst.	M. N. Yakovlev
Meat production	Prof.	F. P. Polovinkin
Refrigeration	Inst.	K. P. Tokhotsky
Agric. Economy	Prof.	N. P. Nikitin
Organization of Agriculture	"	M. N. Vonzblein
Agric. Bookkeeping Experiments	Inst.	A. A. Levitsky
Social Measures in Animal Husbandry	Prof.	E. F. Liskun
Dairy Cooperatives	Inst.	A. P. Yurmaliat

He has fulfilled all the practical assignments required by the curriculum in the disciplines listed.

In order to fully complete his special training in cattle and dairy farming he has still to present a satisfactorily written thesis in his field of expertise.

Rector — M. Fofanova

Members of the Board — P. Kuleshov

Od. Polovinkin

Secretary — (signature)

Stamp with the RSFSR seal

Mosgublit 4690. Moscow. Edition 100 cop. Mosc. Poligr. Printers' Assoc., B. Lubyanka, 16, tel. 4-83-23

Simple arithmetic: of forty-three disciplines, only two were social. And the professors: look how many of them there were and of what caliber. Sergei Vavilov became president of the Academy of Sciences. Ivan Popov became head of Father's department at Timiryazev. Yakovlev was his guardian angel for life. Some I remember on the spines of books. One professor, I heard, was intimidated into informing: for years he betrayed people and suffered remorse. About most of them I know nothing, though there is undoubtedly something...

Having graduated from the institute Father devoted all his energies to *Chudakovo/Rodniki*. He managed a significant profit and was noticed, as was his almost proletarian origin: soon he was being groomed to manage a vast nationalized estate. But he didn't want to leave: across the Makedonka in Udelnaya, Father and his brother Ivan had built a dacha in '26. That had used up the last of the tsarist 10-ruble gold pieces at the chervonets rate: nine and a half for ten.

Yakovlev's advice was to quit *Chudakovo* and steer clear of large estates: Defense Commissar Voroshilov had his eye on them. Times were changing: any agricultural worker and teacher was open to attack.

A seemingly innocent piece of paper, even touching:

TO YAKOV ARTEMEVICH SERGEEV

Former manager of the Rodniki Pedigree Stock Farm

We, citizens of the village of Vereya give you, Yakov Artemevich, our profound thanks for your lectures, papers and practical instructions in tending livestock.

Your instructions and advice have not been for naught: they have been of great benefit to us. We learned a lot from you; and we wish to continue the mission you began with our thanks.

(In longhand after the typescript):

From citizens of the village of Vereya, Bykovo Volost, as certified by the Vereya Village Soviet

Chairman Zharkov

12/VIII — '26

Two or three years later this piece of paper could have landed you in labor camp: *the mission you began, Sergeev's mission.* Timiryazev professors were suddenly kulak ideologists because of Sunday lectures they had read to peasants.

CERTIFICATE

The Beetrootcenter's local trade union committee hereby certifies that agronomist and cattle-breeder comrade Sergeev, Ya. A., the whole time he worked at the Beetrootcenter from 20 April 1926 to 1 May 1930, did volunteer work through the Trade Union, first as the united local trade union committee's acting delegate, then through the local trade union committee's organization at the Beetrootcenter as the elected secretary (part-time, unpaid) of the latter, which post he occupied until recently.

Concurrently with the duties specified, comrade Sergeev was at various times authorized representative of the Agrosection, authorized representative of the Mutual Aid Fund, and collector of membership dues both for the Trade Union and for the latter organizations.

Father tried to seem and to be like everyone else. The main thing was to blend into the background, not to stand out. The moustache was gone for good, on his head he wore a cap, his long belted blouse was rumpled, his jacket worn. In photographs taken at a spa in '29, he is wearing white trousers and a white open-necked shirt — the way everyone else did at spas in those days. His expression is invariably good-natured.

Though younger, his brother Ivan is wearing a pique shirt whose collar fastens at the side and a good suit, a refined-looking pince-nez and a neat moustache: his appearance is even foppish, but his expression is gloomy.

He too had been a volunteer in the First World War. Father

was lucky to have lost his rank. During a purge, volunteer Ivan was counted as a White officer — they were trying to sniff them out then — and imprisoned. Panic-stricken, Avdotia divorced her enemy of the people. But Ivan was soon released, and they remarried. Still, Ivan couldn't get his book, *Breeding Farm Animals*, published until Father added his name to the title page.

The eldest, Pavel, had it hardest of all: throughout the '20s he had worked in the town of Dmitrov, in — oh, horrors! — a cooperative. The Dmitrov cooperative had existed since 1915. Prince Kropotkin, hounded out of Moscow, had had a hand in it between 1918 and 1920. Pavel was rounded up during collectivization's first swipe. Fortunately, his sentence was survivable.

Father, like everyone else, was hauled in for questioning. At one interrogation they played the silent game all day. Investigator Lastochkin wrote questions on scraps of paper, Father wrote answers. Towards evening Father read:

"Do you plead guilty to harboring pedigree horses?"

Sound of mind, Father burst out laughing: he'd never had anything to do with pedigree horses. Lastochkin turned nasty, waved his revolver and threatened, but let him go. A few years later Father ran into Lastochkin at a conference: he had come up in the world on pedigree horses and was introducing himself as a professor of horse breeding from Krasnodar.

A checked sheet of copybook paper:

3 January 1933

CERTIFICATE

Given to Yakov Artemevich Sergeev in that he does truly come from a poor peasant family in the village of Zhukovka in the Dmitrov district of the Moscow region.

Sergeev's parents never had any hired labor and did not engage in trade.

Chairman of the Village Soviet (signature)
Secretary (signature)
Official stamp.

On an official form with a bluish grid:

CERTIFICATE OF MARRIAGE (reissue)

Citizen Sergeev, Yakov Artemevich, and citizeness Mikhailova, Evgenia Ivanovna, entered into marriage on 23/I — 1933, which was duly recorded as entry No. 326 in the registry book of civil marriages on the 23rd of January in the year 1933, to which signature and stamp attest.

After registration, the husband retained the surname Sergeev, the wife Mikhailova.
Place of registration: Dzerzhinsky District Registry Office, Moscow.

Date of issue 3/VI. 1949. 11 — A No. 661952.

Dzerzhinsky District Registry Office means that in 1933 Father had already moved from Chistye Prudy to Kapelsky Lane; reissue means that marriage licenses were required only in special cases in the early '30s.

On a flimsy slip of paper, roughly one quarter of a copybook page:

RSFSR	CERTIFICATE
Registry Office	I witnessed the birth
Dzerzhinsky Dist.	of Sergeev, Andrei
27 June 1933	3/VI — '33
No. 3482	(signature)
Moscow	Official stamp

The day I was born, 3 June 1933, Fyodor Gladkov wrote from Moscow to Andrei Bely in Koktebel:

> Here we have lost the sun. For the last ten days or so we've had dank cold, wet fog, continuous rain, and gloom. I want to go away, but I can't: Party purge and volunteer work.

I was born the year Hitler came to power, the year the Belomor Canal was finished, the year of the Ukraine's most terrible famine.

Food was scarce in Moscow, too. Mama wouldn't touch potatoes and so lived on rutabagas alone:

"You're my rutabagan boy..."

Father had no gold to exchange at the Foreign Trade Store for proper food.

"I was weak," said Mama, "hemoglobin was 38 percent."

After she had me, Mama didn't work anywhere. Father joked:

"Andrei has a high-priced nanny, university-educated."

A homemade photograph: Papa and Mama in Udelnaya standing by a haystack, nice young faces. But Father seems never to have mastered photography: his pictures, too, are like everyone else's — accidental murk, 9 x 12 cm.

A long business trip to Orenburg. In the train Father opened a faded political pamphlet. The other man in his compartment — there were just the two of them — grabbed it out of his hands:

"Lenin... Oh, I thought it was Trotsky or somebody..."

The man turned out to be a State executioner:

"You lead him down a corridor, but he doesn't know anything. At a certain point you shoot him in the back of the head. He falls through a hole in the floor. And you do that every day, maybe thirty times. I'm dead tired. Going to my mother's for a rest..."

In telling this story, Father expressed neither surprise nor horror: that's how it should be, we have a dictatorship, we don't hide the fact.

He always slept soundly, but in '37 and '38, he told us, he woke up every time a car stopped outside or late-night steps sounded on the stairs. Again like everyone else, but he was threatened by something specific. At work, the Dymans informed. They also called on us at home. Their interest in Father might be pure as the driven snow — or then again....

On 1 October 1937 the Academy of Socialist Agriculture assigned Father — as it had for years — 360 hours of work at an associate professor's salary.

On 5 October 1937 Father was relieved of his associate professorship in connection with a decrease in teaching hours for the 1937/38 academic year.

In his painstaking, arthritic longhand, Pavel Aleksandrovich Raushenbach, an honest German, wrote a saving

TESTIMONIAL

I have known associate professor Sergeev, Yakov Arteme-vich, since 1930 when I came to work with him in the Alimentation Department of the former Institute of Meat-and-Dairy Cattle Breeding, later known as the Moscow Zootechnical Institute named after Molotov. The Zootechnical Institute was eventually combined with the Zootechnical Department of Timiryazev Agricultural Academy. Thus our joint work continued over the course of this time in the Farm Animal Alimentation Department. Throughout this period no one ever cast aspersions on the academic work of comrade Sergeev, Yakov Artemevich, on the contrary he was always considered a good teacher, his attitude towards his work was always highly conscientious, and he was well-liked by the students. Besides his teaching work, comrade Sergeev was always conducting research and applying it to production. Comrade Sergeev was a good social activist and took on a great deal of volunteer work most years. I consider comrade Sergeev a highly experienced worker, both as a teacher and a researcher, moreover I regard him as a good comrade who gets on well with his colleagues.

If the All-Union Academy of Socialist Agriculture loses comrade Sergeev then it will be to the Alimentation Department's detriment in that if a new teacher has to be hired to continue this work he may be less qualified and less suited from the point of view of teaching and conducting research.

In conclusion, I would like to emphasize that Sergeev, Yakov Artemevich, is currently carrying out a large project intended for the defense of his dissertation for a Candidate's degree in agriculture.

16/III — '38 Prof. Raushenbach

Raushenbach was very old and very tall. He was always fishing fistfuls of almonds out of his left-hand jacket pocket:

"Do have some. Six nuts after every meal and you will never have any trouble with your stomach."

Father was reinstated. The pattern: Raushenbach's selflessly brave t e s t i m o n i a l — plus the intervention, no doubt, of the unfailing Yakovlev, by then a full professor.

It is easy to imagine what people said about Yakovlev, a thriving man with a dangerous past, a strange omniscience and an incomprehensible power. It was also irritating that after a cancer operation, he had not, like other people, kicked the bucket, but turned around and married a much younger woman and lived with her for fifteen years.

Walking home from the funeral, Papa slowly summed up:

"He was a good man."

In Mama's opinion, Father could have been a full professor, too:

"It was all Popov's doin', dishonorable he was. Afraid of the competition. He knew languages, enough to scrape together a Doctor's dissertation. Father didn't know any. And Popov held him back. Your father put up with everythin'. His colleagues couldn't believe how much patience he had. He learned it in the Army."

Father disagreed — not because he so valued and respected Popov. Father never thought of himself as a scholar, he was just a researcher, that's what he wrote, that's what he said. He also said that he liked productive work.

He was listed as an associate professor in the alimentation department as of 15/I — 1932.

His title of associate professor was confirmed on 19 March 1935.

He completed a night course at Marxist-Leninist University on 28 March 1935.

He received the reviews of his dissertation on 29 August 1939 — just after the Soviet-German Pact.

He received an honorary award from the Soviet Agricultural Society for active and fruitful work on 31 August 1939 — the day the Japanese pulled back from the Halhin-Gol River and the eve of World War Two.

He defended his Candidate's dissertation on 10 September when Warsaw was already defending itself.

He received his Candidate's degree in agricultural science for his dissertation on *The Composition and Calorie Content of Consistent Additional Weight in Pigs Fattened for Meat and Lard* on 1 October 1939 — after the annexation of Western Ukraine and Western Byelorussia and just before his fiftieth birthday.

Father's health had always been enviable. But in 1937-38, on top of that *unpleasantness*, he was laid low by Udelnaya malaria — every summer he took cinchona, quinine, and quinacrine, and looked yellow. The year before the war — for the second and last time — he went to the Crimea for a rest. He sent me a postcard with a Genoese tower.

Amateur photographs — Father's own and other people's. Young looking, sturdily-built, smiling pleasantly at the camera. A warm — wadded — coat with a wide astrakhan collar, an astrakhan hat. A cap, an unassuming jacket and vest, a knotted tie. Or in glasses and a white smock standing next to some test tubes and a microscope.

His Sunday suit looks almost like his everyday one. A man with nothing special about him — a man like everyone else.

The trouble was they were collaring everyone. His official work record — despite his Candidate's degree and countless accompanying certificates — breaks off on 3/1V — '39. And picks up five years later: on 1/X — '44. In 1940, again on Yakovlev's advice, Father took himself out of harm's way, out of Timiryazev, and ran the animal husbandry department at the Moscow Agronomist's Club — away from anyone who knew him — in suburban Dolgoprudnaya.

He rode the suburban train to work. In October of '41 he left Dolgoprudna on foot half an hour before the Germans took it.

He never talked much about the war, he accepted it. He often sang with feeling:

> Calm yourself, take this shawl,
> Your son will come home to all.

The first winter of the war, he lost a pood. His jacket hung on him, his trousers bagged. Father didn't complain, rather he made light of it.

His brother Pavel sometimes came to us from Dmitrov:

"One day we eat meat, the next day mushrooms, the third day vegetables."

Once he brought us a piece of lard, another time, a jar of boiled mushrooms.

We were saved by Professor Osolchuk — one of the inventors of Soviet Champagne, it seems, and a Stalin laureate. He gave Father an enormous bottle of pure alcohol. We diluted the alcohol with water and traded it for food.

During the summer of '42, thanks to some extraordinary wangling, Father went practically every day to the village of Panki where he received milk and sour cream from the State farm there in return for lectures he hadn't given.

Steady relative prosperity began with a "Research Workers" ration card and registration at a special store in Moscow near Petrovskiye Vorota. The food issued there was much better: instead of meat, say, they gave you not herring but Siberian salmon or red caviar. Before the special store, Father had gone for a whole summer to an RW cafeteria in Sport, a restaurant on Leningrad Avenue. Usually they let you take food home.

In lean times Father grumbled at Mama's improvidence:

"You never make anything last; you always eat up whatever there is!"

Mama made excuses:

"Can't bear the temptation."

Grandfather died of dystrophy. Papa cried. They hadn't been on good terms at the end. I knew this and asked:

"Why are you crying?"

"People cry at funerals because they're sorry for themselves."

My sober, energetic father had little interest in the dead. He watched over the old women who had been his colleagues in the '20s. During the famine he always brought them something from his garden. Mama scoffed:

"Yakov cottons to old women."

Yet Father never once went himself and never took me to the Vyalki cemetery where his mother (Granny Ksenia) was buried.

According to Certificate No. 930, Father was discharged from military service altogether on 23 February 1918.

His *personal record*, begun in '23, ends this way: *Taken off the rolls 12/IX — '30 because of having reached the age limit of forty.*

On 21 June 1943 the Krasnopolyansky (Agronomist's Club) district enlistment office pronounced him fit for service as a noncombatant according to Art. 31, para. 1 — at age fifty-four. Still, they never sent him to the frontlines.

Father's brother Pavel missed being sent because of his age, Ivan and Kirill because of illness. Kirill — Uncle Kira — came to visit before the war with his wife and little girl. The little girl stamped her foot on our small floor and demanded that the butter for her bread be cut in the shape of a diamond.

"Snippy little whippersnapper," Mama concluded behind her back. And about Kirill:

"The most sensitive of all the Sergeevs. Only he's kind of strange: tells you somethin' sad then starts to giggle."

By now Kirill had been evacuated to Sarapul. A line from one of his letters: *I've got myself a Stalin cow (a goat).* The envelope was stamped: *Checked by military censorship.*

He fell ill in Sarapul. Granny got him into Sklifosovsky Hospital. The surgeon opened him up then sewed him up: inoperable. From my journal:

UNCLE KIRA DIED
27 February 1944

Having sat out the most dangerous time in the countryside, Father was back in Moscow in '44, at the Chemotechnical Institute of Meat Production, and again at Timiryazev as of early '46.

Like everyone else, he worked from morning till night, and every year two months' salary was deducted as a "loan" to the government.

Everything was fine even. In '44, he received a medal *for the defense of Moscow, in '46 for valiant labor in the Great Patriotic War*. In May of '49 — for his twenty-five years of teaching to date — he began receiving, in addition to his salary, an academic pension of 250 rubles a month. In '51, he received an Order of the Red Banner of Labor, and in '54 an All-Union Exhibition of Agriculture medal.

Time was divided: winters on Kapelsky, summers in Udelnaya. Seeing how lonely I was, Papa gladly went with me to the cinema, and the theater. My first plays were *She Stoops to Conquer* and *Long Ago* at the Red Army Theater. In summer, on Kuznetsky Most in Moscow, Father would buy me as many stamps as he could so as to give them to me piecemeal in Udelnaya, over several visits — but he could never hold back. When duplicates turned up, or stamps I didn't need, I felt an excruciating gratitude —- the needless present touched me as a demonstration of profound love and attention devoid of interest and worth.

Very early Papa taught me photography using a *Photokor* and prewar plates; in '46 he bought me a FED at a second-hand store.

In the winter of '47 we spent a long time in that same store choosing a *wireless*, and finally chose a wonderful *Telefunken*.

In '48 Papa took me on an excursion to Leningrad.

That summer he gave me a Kharkov bicycle: he didn't trust the trophy ones. We took the electric train to the Moscow Trade Store in Marina Roshcha and were fined for unlawful carriage on the way back. At Udelnaya Papa, to my amazement, got on the bicycle and rode off. I spent not a few days learning, counted poles and ditches. My fear of people, my constraint, had kept me from borrowing bicycles and learning at the proper time.

Sometimes, in anger, Papa called me a hot-house flower, a prim little miss. He was always trying to chase me out of doors: he didn't succeed until maybe '46. He tried to teach me to swim: I more or less taught myself. Several times he tried to teach me to skate: in vain. I must have hit my head at some point: for many, many years I was afraid of the winter — afraid that it would be slippery and that I would fall. I had two concussions: in '49 and in '51 or '52.

I grew and our room became more cramped. After the war, Papa again began setting money aside for a swap — and lost it when the ruble was devalued tenfold in '47. Papa didn't lament and again put part of his pay in the savings bank. The rest of the money he kept at home — we knew where, it wasn't under lock and key. That's probably why I never once helped myself. When I asked, Papa always gave me what I needed without any questions:

"Without money a man is a good-for-nothing."

He encouraged my independent purchases:

"Good. You didn't have that coin. That's a history book."

He never did manage to swap our 13-square-meter room. In the summer of '53 he was given a 17-square-meter room in a Timiryazev apartment — on Chapayev Lane, near Novopeschanaya Street. The people who moved into the other room didn't make especially nice neighbors and Mama, naturally, didn't get on with them. She grumbled:

"An' all because he's such a pushover. Could've snapped up the whole apartment."

It wasn't Stalin's death, but my age and education that triggered my political outbursts. Papa — on walks at home or in Udelnaya — would hear me out with an irritable look and then explain:

"But we don't hide the fact that we have a dictatorship. It's that fool of a tsar who's to blame, wouldn't give the people a responsible ministry. That's all they asked: give us a ministry responsible to the Duma... Under the tsar, I would have had my own house... If he'd lived, Lenin wouldn't have done away with the New Economic Policy or started collectivization. You know what he wrote about Stalin in his testament? 'This cook may concoct a spicy dish...' Destroyed the entire intelligentsia. A marvelous intelligentsia it was... But in the summer of '17, Russia had the greatest freedom of any country in the world. The war was on, and at meetings people from all different parties spoke out. And you had your pick of newspapers..."

Father didn't trust the *Voice of America* or the *BBC*. He found it demeaning to have to read between the lines in the papers. Since what had happened had happened, the thing to do was not to dig in your heels, but to accept it. He accepted, dutifully and outwardly, all the required forms and formulas:

"And he calls himself a Soviet man... and he calls himself a Komsomol member... and he calls himself a Party member..."

At the end of '51 I was holding forth at the dinner table about the Estonians: that summer the three of us had come into Moscow from the dacha to see a performance by the touring Estonia theater. I was trying to see the Baltics as an alternative to the Soviet system, and the Estonians really did sing well. Mama was thrilled:

"An' Tiit Kuuzik at the ball — the way he caught Olga up, an' sang, an' danced — he was better even than our Khokhlov!"

I was holding forth about the Estonians, and suddenly Papa said:

"Want to see the card of a certain Estonian?" and he took a brand new Party card out of his drawer. I was dumbstruck.

Mama hid the fact from family and friends:

"Mother told me to watch out an' not breathe a word, never know what might happen. If somethin' does happen, they'll be strung up from the first lamppost..."

A decade later, in a little forest beyond Chudakovo, I heard how it had happened.

While I was finishing school, applying to the Cinema Institute, and boasting of my various involvements, Papa was being hauled into Lubyanka. Almost like a job: once a week for the whole day. They were trying to recruit him: his reputation was too good. For years he had used the trade union to stand up for students and teachers, they all came to him for advice. He was the perfect person to act as an informer. Father didn't know how to get rid of them. They were threatening him. He asked someone on the Party bureau at Timiryazev what to do. His unknown savior said he needed to quickly ruin his own reputation by applying to join the Party — he'd often been asked to join, after all — because what student or teacher would bare their soul to a Party member? Father applied — and the secret police backed off.

He trusted me; without asking, he trusted my ventures — the Cinema Institute, the Foreign Languages Institute, my precarious profession of translator. He would have preferred me to become a scientist with graduate degrees and a solid income, but he never objected and only occasionally asked:

"Have any work?"

Lyuda and I were married in the fall of '57. Father was against our living the four of us in one room, but we couldn't find anything to rent, so we spent our last winter together on Chapayev.

The following summer in Udelnaya, Father registered Lyuda's parents as living at our dacha and wangled permission to build a small addition there. But because of the disparity in our natural alliances, the arrangement ended stormily, in an all-night shouting match and my leaving.

Lyuda and I rented whatever turned up, rooms, parts of rooms, ten places in four years, on sufferance. We had no money and for a long time Father helped us. Lyuda never visited my parents. A reconciliation occurred when we moved into a cooperative apartment paid for by Papa — 46,864 old rubles.

But when things went wrong between Lyuda and me, Father — mainly because of his granddaughter — did the impermissible and the unforgivable in an effort to bring me back to my former home and prevent a new marriage.

On the 16th of October 1959, the rector of Timiryazev, Loza, congratulated Father on his seventieth birthday.

In 1960 Papa received a registration certificate from the Inventions and Discoveries Committee for his work on *The Dietary Properties of Certain Feeds and Rations Given to Cattle.*

It was a Doctor's dissertation ready-made. On top of fifty publications. Popov was by now an academician and — even Mama said so — would not have interfered. But Father demurred: too many had collapsed under the pressure.

"I have enough to do as it is."

Papa retired on a 120-ruble pension on 9/II/'62, but on the 1st of September he turned up for work. On his office door there was still the nameplate Yakov A. SERGEEV: Khrushchev had threatened to disband the academy and the young scientists were fleeing.

Timiryazev had always been a thorn in the government's side. Chayanov and Kondratev had balked at collectivization. Before the war, Pryanishnikov had insisted on nominating his former student, the recently arrested Nikolai Vavilov, for the first Stalin Prize. The pseudoscientific word of Lysenko was not law at Timiryazev where they had once received a frightened letter from Czechoslovakia: experiments there were not producing Lysenko-type results — what should they do? At an academic session in Kiev, Khrushchev was reviling the experts when Professor Chizhevsky called out from his seat: "We still need to figure out who's to blame for the collapse of agriculture in the Ukraine!"

Khrushchev decided to send Timiryazev packing. Polyansky took the rector, the Party secretary, the union chairman and several professors out to a swampy place a hundred kilometers from Moscow:

"Your academy will be here."

Professor Kolesnev, Samuil Georgievich, a Jew, flew at him: "No it won't!"

"Then we'll close you down."

"The tsar wanted to close us down and he couldn't. You'll fare that much worse."

Polyansky said nothing and left. Papa told the story several times, as a legend.

The morning after Khrushchev's fall, Brezhnev summoned Timiryazev's rector and assured him of his love and respect.

As a pensioner Papa was never at loose ends: people visited — by telephone at least — every day. He and Fofanova — sitting pretty after her disgrace under Stalin — called each other on holidays. There was always something to do: food to be bought, Party meetings to be attended at the academy (it would have been awkward not to go, besides he wanted to see everyone and catch up), events i n t o w n.

"Perhaps there's an exhibit?"

He was drawn to things that were h i s t o r i c a l, c o n t e m p o r a r y, m a t c h l e s s.

He went to the nearby *Leningrad* cinema. When a chamber music theater opened by the Sokol metro station, Papa became a regular, especially since the woman in the box-office was a neighbor on Chapayev Lane.

I'm ashamed to say that after Granny died Papa and Mama began to get along and live happily. Every spring they set off for Udelnaya and lived there like o l d - f a s h i o n e d l a n d o w n e r s. They discussed the changing weather, months, seasons:

"Peter and Paul less an hour's all." (12 July)

"Ilya the Prophet takes two from it." (2 August)

"It's begun to get dark so early..."

A bag slung over his shoulder, Papa walked to the station — to the open-air market, the shops, the stalls: they all knew him — for milk, bread, butter. As always, he dug in the garden till late in the fall. For anything more strenuous — turning up the earth, mixing the fertilizer, scattering pine needles — he hired tramps. Mama scorned them. But Papa was always respectful and equable: he was the boss. He wasn't afraid to give them money upfront — for a drink — a ruble or even three.

It was my job to go out to Udelnaya several times every spring to sow, to plant, to prune the apple trees. We would go for the whole day, air the dacha, go to the neighbors for water and drink tea with Mama's sandwiches. Papa luxuriated. Sitting on the veranda with the windows thrown open, he marveled:

"What a divine hush!"

Taking a sandwich out of its newspaper wrapping, he would recall the inscription carved on the wooden bread basket in Usolye — BREAD AT TABLE: HANDS ABLE — and again marvel.

He marveled that, coming out of the metro by the Lenin Museum, he had suddenly caught sight of the handsome Grand Hotel, and when it was demolished, he marveled at the House of Unions behind it, its columns in all their glory.

He marveled over that wonderful i n v e n t i o n, the radio.

To the end of his life he marveled over *Eugene Onegin* and read it every night before bed.

Once he and Galya were picking plums. Papa oohed and ahed over every one, how exquisite. Galya asked:

"Yakov Artemevich, what's more important to you, your harvest or your pleasure?"

"Well, not my harvest..." — and he chuckled.

Against the winter, tucked under the porch roof where no cat could get at it, he would leave the titmice a battered pot of birdseed and a big piece of lard. When he came out to check on the dacha in winter, he would pour out more seed, put up more lard.

Every evening he went for a walk on Chapayev — along the edge of the park. Once from behind a bush a boy asked him:

"Old man, ain't you afraid someone'll knock yer block off?"

"No. What could they steal? It's all old."

He wasn't afraid — but he was surprised — when a vicious dog came at him:

"What are you, mad?"

His sense of his own self-worth — having survived the '20s and '30s — never failed him.

He wasn't one to rack his brains over insoluble problems, but the problems at hand he always solved and always by himself. When Mama came down with pneumonia in Udelnaya, he nursed her through the summer.

"For once in her life she at least had a rest from cooking. Better than a holiday."

The Sergeev brothers were dying in ascending order — beginning with the youngest. Pavel went out of turn: ahead of Papa.

In the spring of '75 Papa was operated on by the best surgeon. More destructive than the incision was the anaesthetic. He tossed in his hospital bed for days, tried to get up and walk out, other patients had to hold him back. In a sensible voice he admonished them:

"Why are you using force?"

He never did remember that Galya had come to see him.

That summer he and Mama lived in Udelnaya. On October 29, New Style, the four of us celebrated his eighty-sixth birthday.

For years I'd been proudly saying:

"My father's eighty, and he's healthier than I am..."

"My father's eighty-five, and he's..."

On the 8th of December he collected his pension at the savings bank and bought food for the week. That evening he joked with a little girl in his entrance: she had painted her nails blue.

At one in the morning he got up:

"Zhenia, something's wrong with me. Fetch me the nitroglycerin."

Mama doesn't remember calling the ambulance, or being visited by her friend from next-door, a woman doctor:

"You've already done everything that can be done..."

The afternoon of the 9th Galya and I came home from the movies to find a note stuck in the door: *Yakov Artemevich is dead.* The urgent telegram came later.

Papa hadn't been to see a doctor in months, so an autopsy was done. The attending physician was amazed:

"What didn't they write down... Diseases like that don't occur at his age. Your father died of old age."

We spent the night at Mama's. I lay down on Papa's couch: it drew me. I wanted to slip my feet into Papa's slippers.

Surprisingly many of the old Timiryazev guard, themselves with one foot in the grave, came to the morgue for the funeral. Up in front, the Dymans cried. Delegates from the Party/trade union committee accompanied the body to the crematorium along with friends of Galya's and mine who had never met him.

The department sent a letter:

> Dear Evgenia Ivanovna and Andrei Yakovlevich,
>
> A great sorrow has befallen you. In times of such sorrow it is hard, even impossible, to find words of comfort.
>
> Yakov Artemevich worked in the academy's Alimentation Department for 36 years. The department has lost a comrade and a friend loved by all.
>
> Yakov Artemevich was a man of great modesty, great diligence and great integrity. He treated all members of the department as equals, regardless of their position, and always addressed them simply and directly. He was loved by the many

students to whom he passed on his rich zootechnical and educational experience.

He was demanding, strict and fair.

Yakov Artemevich's research work showed him to be a principled scientist, regardless of the circumstances.

In this posthumous letter, we in the department wish to remember once again the oldest teacher at the Academy, on the zootechnical faculty and in the alimentation department, and say to him: "Rest in peace, dear friend and comrade, you will always be in our hearts."

Six signatures. Possibly including that of the unknown savior who advised Papa to quickly ruin his own reputation.

Mama was forever saying — to me, to herself, to the walls:

"Father was a good man," and burying her face in her handkerchief.

But I had long since realized that my father — by virtue of having been true to himself, by virtue of his health and of rare coincidences — was one of those least sullied by the time in which he lived.

In deliberate solitude I buried the urn in Nikolo-Arkhangelsk cemetery. The urn seemed warm: I kept hugging it to me, or was I hugging myself to it?

BOLSHAYA EKATERININSKAYA

When Grandfather turned eighteen, the matchmaker asked for his photograph.

He and a friend clubbed together and had their picture taken on Tverskaya Street: an elegant studio portrait with columns, and cypresses in the background. The friend was c o m m o n, Grandfather was n o t: he was stately, with an elongated face, a moustache, a French crop and fashionable striped trousers.

You would never have known that he was no one from nowhere: the obscure village of Shilovo, in Ruza Uyezd. That he had grown up in someone else's hut and had smallpox on the stove-bench: the pockmarks had been smoothed out in the photograph. That from the age of eight he had lived in the city as an apprentice, which included fetching vodka — for others at first, later for himself, too. That his idea of amusement was:

"A dandy came strolling down the street in a straw hat. We threw a cucumber pickle at him — hit his pince-nez! He had to feel around on the ground for it, couldn't see a thing: we burst out laughing, and ran for it!"

"In winter we went out for fisticuffs on the Moscow River."

In Granny's hand on the back of the elegant studio portrait: *1891.* According to their internal passports, Grandfather was born in 1876, Granny in 1886. In fact, Granny was a year younger than Grandfather. Mama was born in 1898. For the solution to this problem, turn to pages 146 and 172.

Photographs of Granny done up in inconceivable *fin de siècle*: guilloches, fancy hats, muffs. On the back of the passe-partout are medals and:

Photograph by Trunov in Moscow. Court photographer of HIS MAJESTY THE SHAH OF PERSIA, HIS MAJESTY THE KING OF SERBIA, HIS HIGHNESS THE ARCHDUKE OF AUSTRIA, HIS HIGHNESS THE PRINCE OF MONTENEGRO AND HIS HIGHNESS THE CROWN PRINCE OF SWEDEN AND NORWAY.

Her face, however, is plain with high cheekbones. In her village — Ozherelye, near Kashira — they called her the Mordvinian.

"They also called me a forest girl. I wasn't scared in the forest. Once I met a tramp and darted into the bushes. Catch me if you can! I was reckless, afraid of nothing. I dove down deep underwater. I could fish the littlest thing up from the riverbed: with my toes, as if they were fingers. Whenever anyone dropped anything in it was always: Arisha will get it. But the fields scared me. In the fields there was nowhere to hide."

According to a family legend, Granny's granny h a d   b e e n c a u g h t   u p   b y   a   G y p s y once in a field. Granny's brother Semyon was dark and swarthy: a Gypsy. Granny herself had a second daughter, Tonya, just like him: a Gypsy. Her whole life, Mama g y p p e d people.

In Ozherelye, of the Kalabushkin family there survived only:

Ekaterina (Great Aunt Katya): the feeble-minded eldest;

Semyon (Great Uncle Semyon): the Gypsy, a self-made man;

Irina (Arisha): my grandmother;

Vassa (Greant Aunt Asya): the kindest one;

Fedosia (Great Aunt Fenia): the family beauty.

Their mother was wet nurse to a merchant family, the Trubnikovs. Arisha was the first to follow her to Moscow — to that grand, rich house. Never mind the house, the whole lane it seems was theirs: Trubnikovsky.

Arisha would be sent to the larder for some jam. She: "A spoonful into the bowl, a spoonful into my mouth, a spoonful into the bowl, a spoonful into my mouth. But I was scared. Old lady Trubnikova was always saying: 'Your eyes are pits, your hands are rakes; what your eyes spy, your hands snatch.' Even so I ate my fill, like Danila. There was this man who lived all alone in Ozherelye. 'Don't give me a little,' he always said. 'Give me so much I won't be able to hold any more for a whole year.'"

The jam was kept in earthenware jars. Once Arisha opened one — and found some gold coins: old lady Trubnikova had squirreled them away from everyone and then forgotten. Gold coins were not jam, mustn't touch. But then finery was like jam. Once Arisha and the other girls, without a twinge of conscience, dressed up in their mistresses' gowns, went walking up the boulevard towards Pushkin's statue — and ran right into the young Trubnikovs. But they only laughed, they didn't tell the old lady.

"They were cultured... Anastasy Aleksandrovich was a good man, courteous, gallant. He was an aesthete, he wrote articles... Lived in Paris most of the time... His mother was forever muttering about him squandering his father's capital..."

Anastasy Aleksandrovich came home in fine fettle one night after midnight. Katya opened the door for him (Arisha had prevailed on the Trubnikovs to take her, too). Anastasy Aleksandrovich:

"Merci bien! Merci bien! Mille fois merci!"

Katya burst into tears. The Trubnikovs tried to comfort her:

"But he didn't mean any harm."

"Oh, no! He swore at me."

Ridiculous as the incident was, it was beyond Katya's powers of understanding and the old lady showed her the door.

The Trubnikovs enrolled Arisha — o n e o f t h e f a m i l y — in Brodsky's medical courses to study for four years. The courses were on Third Meshchanskaya Street, just a stone's throw from Bolshaya Ekaterininskaya.

Life at the Trubnikovs would have been fine, if not for the old lady. At seventeen, Granny said to the milkmaid: "Find me a husband, only one that's a gentleman."

She kicked up a fuss at first about Grandfather: pockmarks. The milkmaid comforted her:

> Handsome is as handsome does,
> And pocks are not the worst that was.

They were married at the church of Old Pimen.

Mama: "At the wedding, Grandfather had your Granny given away by — you won' believe by who — by a Jew! Knopp..."

Knopp's blessing — an icon of the Savior in the style of Vasnetsov — has survived to this day.

They began living on Bolshaya Ekaterininskaya Street. The little wooden houses often burned. After the marriage their papers were consumed in a fire. An orphan, Grandfather had never known his real last name; sometimes he was listed as Martynov, other times as Kochnov. Now Grandfather and Granny registered for good under new last names derived from their patronymics: Ivan Mikhailovich Mikhailov and — in the noble manner — Irina Nikitichna Nikitina-Mikhailova. This was the first point at which their dates of birth could have been altered.

Granny about another fire:

"We had just returned after the summer: we hung the icon of Nikolai the Miracle-worker in the corner and piled our bundles under him and behind the furniture. Suddenly a fire broke out on the second floor. Firemen flooded it. The water seeped down to the first floor, the wallpaper came off the walls in curls and covered up all our belongings. Thieves looked in and didn't see anything. But they robbed the other tenants blind..."

With a different intonation:

"A thief broke in, stole a suit and left a note:

> Your suit won't warm you in winter,
> In summer it's too hot to wear."

This was considered the height of wit on Bolshaya Ekaterininskaya.

The streets off and around Bolshaya Ekaterininskaya formed a working-class settlement, a square framed by the St Katharine Institute, Tryphonovskaya and Third Meshchanskaya streets and Samara Lane. A village except for the straightness of the lines in which the houses stood and their stuccoed facades.

There were two sites — on the diagonal — to see: the ancient church of Tryphon the Martyr on Tryphonovskaya Street and, on Samara Lane, a wooden house in the Empire style that had belonged to Count Osterman-Tolstoy.

Bolshaya Ekaterininskaya was a world unto itself. People went in town to visit relatives or to attend church on high holidays. On Sundays in warm weather at tables under the trees they would play: chess (with self-importance); old man's sixty-six (in earnest); and bingo (with flourishes).

"Two smackers!"

"There 'n' backer!"

Boys of all ages raced pigeons from the roofs.

As a young man, Grandfather brawled, drank himself quickly and horribly drunk, and dreamed violent dreams:

"Of ripping a policeman's guts out..."

"Of pulling some black coat's long hair..."

He got his chance during the Moscow uprising of 1905. A metalworker and union member, Grandfather tore lampposts out of the ground in the Presnia district. Granny brought him food.

The experience sobered him up fast and for the rest of his life. He drank less, grew gentler and read every word of *Russkoye Slovo* (a Sytin paper, it had variety, from Doroshevich to Rozanov and Blok). But he never meddled in anything:

"It's none of our business."

Grandfather knew and loved church singing. He advised people where to go on which high holiday. But after 1905 he and Granny had no thought of church. Only in a difficult moment — what else can I do? — would Granny pray. Instead of church, they now went to the Bolshoi Theater or, more often, to the Zimin to hear Chaliapin, Sobinov and Nezhdanova.

A photograph taken in the spring of 1906 or '07.

Wooden houses and a wooden fence, a brick firewall, an elbow drainpipe. Roofs and trees in the background. In a large yard:

Grandfather — tall, in a hat and three-piece suit — is smiling through a black moustache: the artisan-artist;

Granny's friend Maria Antonovna, striking in a hat with a bow: my future faded nanny Matyonna;

Granny: diminutive, with an ostrich plume and wearing a long cloak;

Mama and Vera in white coats. Tonya, the Gypsy, had already died. She was such a beautiful baby that everyone knew she was not long for this world.

Great Aunt Varya (wife of Great Uncle Semyon, the Gyspy), in black lace and a fur tippet, has deigned to allow us to feast our eyes;

her children: Volodka in a coat with a fur collar, the future collector of Chinese antiquities; and doll-like Margushka;

Great Uncle Semyon, the Gypsy, Mama's godfather, stands aloof, his hands in his pockets. He's wearing a bowler hat and morning coat: the man of affairs. He's clearly a guest here. Once a shepherd, he became Polyakov's valet and went with him to Biarritz where he learned respectability and French. A self-made man, he came up in the world on his own. Polyakov was a doctor and a famous philanthropist. Great Uncle Semyon modeled himself more after Polyakov's brother, a mill-owner and millionaire. Only Great Aunt Varya sometimes said, curling her lip:

"The Kalabushkins are all duffers."

Those who knew Great Uncle Semyon attested:

"A Kalabushkin is a greedybushkin."

Between 1905 and 1914 life went well on Bolshaya Ekaterininskaya.

Grandfather had a good job at Faberge, he made seventy-five rubles a month. People said *there were only two such setters in Moscow. Faberge and Laurier were always trying to lure them away from each other. Laurier asked Grandfather to come to London. How could he go? A strange life, a strange language. The idea scared him to death. Faberge wanted to make him a partner.*

Grandfather didn't want a promotion: he always hated to give orders and make decisions for others. In his work he was an artist:

a pendant of variegated gold with leaves and grasses and flowers made out of little rose-diamonds;

dinner rings with flowers and bows of different semi-precious stones;

dinner rings with c a b o c h o n s — *they don't facet like that nowadays* — with large landscape-like jaspers or with a sparkling, a r t i f i c i a l *love knot.*

His creations cost almost nothing to make at the time: a friend did the drawings, his own labor didn't count, the gold came out of his purse, the stones were quite simple (if diamonds, then little rose-diamonds) and the casts were silver.

In 1942, a mug of milk for me cost us one of four puzzle rings with the J a p a n e s e secret: slip it off, drop it on the table and it came apart. Now it was a curved chain of four links. There was only one way to put the ring back together. If you didn't know it, you'd never guess.

F a b e r g e ended this way. The master-jeweler exploded at the man next to Grandfather. Grandfather — the union member — began packing his chest.

"Please, Ivan Mikhailovich! This is no concern or yours."

"We know, we know whose concern it is."

And he left, for good. He respected himself. He loved his work: holidays oppressed him. Every summer he sent his wife and daughters away to the inexpensive countryside. But three times during those nine years of p e a c e t i m e he sent them to a spa in the south — to the Old Crimea, to Novy Afon and to Yessentuki.

> Mr. Ivan Mikhailovich Mikhailov
> Upper trading stalls No. 102
> 1st Jewelers Association. Moscow.
> 1910, 3 July, the Caucasus.

> Dear Papa,
> We received your letter of 2 July and are very glad that all is well with you. Vera and I go to the baths every other day and my kidneys are a little better. We spend whole days sitting in

the park. Vera is expecting 1 ruble from you for her birthday. I weighed myself and I am 1 pood 36 lbs. Vera is 1 pood 17 lbs and Mama is 2 poods 39 lbs. Vassa hasn't weighed herself yet. We all kiss you.

Zhenia

After the St Nicholas Orphan-Asylum (Why an asylum? Not for lack of means!) they wanted to send Mama — who was so c l e v e r — to boarding school. (Mama had read her fill of Charskaya and wanted none of it.) They chose Samgina's Gymnasium on First Meshchanskaya Street. Granny began telling Mama what to say at the entrance exam. Mama:

"But what about *Down with the tsar and his government?*"

"And *Down with the autookracy?*"

"And *The Odessans will feast in a sumptuous palace?*"

These phrases came from conversations with grown-ups in the yard and from the older girls, as did:

> Poor Pourish seems bemused,
> Bamboozled and confused.

Samgina's Gymnasium, not only the upper classes, was the most valuable, active and successful time of Mama's life.

"I worried all the time: 'I've already learned so much, Mam', how much've we paid.' 'Don't worry, Zhen', a lot more than that.'"

"Scripture was a terrible bore, as bad as Marxism classes later on. The Reverend Father'd ask: 'Have you still not learned the hymns?' 'But, Reverend Father, I can't, they don't rhyme, they're all skimble-skamble.' 'Zhenia, how can you talk like that?' Our Reverend Father was kind..."

"I was at the top of my class. The German teacher, Alma Ivanna Walter, she doted on me. I could rattle on in German. I had three friends — Nadka Pavlova, Lidka Kudryavtseva and Milka Podelskaya — one would be the doctor, one the mother, one the sick daughter, we took turns. We'd converse like that the whole lesson, made the conversations up ourselves. The lazy ones who hadn't learned the dialogue, can't tell you how happy they were: they got by because of us. But we liked it..."

"The French teacher, Monsieur Luque, was always sittin' down beside me and I'd ask him, 'Monsieur Luque, is it true French is the most beautiful language?' 'Oh no, Mistress Mikhailova. The most beautiful language is Portuguese.' "

"I loved to dance, was light on my feet. Had as many partners as you please. At balls the steward always danced with me. I also loved to skate. I was always dashing to the *Union* — the nearest rink..."

> The Board of Lydia Fyodorovna Samgina's accredited gymasium for girls, in Moscow, on account of paragraph 12 of the rules concerning examinations of pupils enrolled in gymnasiums and pro-gymnasiums for girls under the Ministry of Public Instruction, has stipulated that fifth-grade pupil Evgenia Mikhailova be awarded a testimonial and this book for her excellent conduct, her diligence and the excellent progress shown by her during the 1913-1914 academic year.
>
> Moscow, 4 September 1914. No. 388.

Gilt-edged W o l f editions:
Olympus by Petiskus.
The Tsar's Children and their Tutors.
The Poems of Count Aleksei Tolstoy.
"I'd rather they'd given me *Prince Serebryany.*"

On a plain Pavlenkov edition of Lermontov in Mama's schoolgirl script:

From Papa, 9 May 1908, 5 o'clock

On a Sytin edition of Gogol:

For my progress from Mama, 5/III/1909

Granny and Grandfather were ashamed of their crooked handwriting.

They finally settled down in a three-story brick house: No. 5a, Apt. 5. Of their three rooms, they rented one out — as did most people, to help with expenses — to as respectable a person as they could find. Bolshaya Ekaterininskaya was being infiltrated by outsiders.

Lev Pavlovich Nikiforov — who could be more respectable than that? — had been recommended. A Penza landowner, he had given his estate away to the peasants: he was a Tolstoyan, had known Tolstoy. He lived on his translations: John Ruskin, Max Nordau. His wife, Ekaterina Ivanovna Zasulich, was the sister of the terrorist Vera Zasulich. Their sons, professional terrorists all, had perished. One doused himself with kerosene in prison and burned to death, another killed the prison warden and was shot on the spot, a third was hung after the Lena River massacre.

The Nikiforovs deposited their things in their room then went out somewhere. Mama ran to the keyhole. From out of a wicker chest — as tall as a man — something red was oozing: terrorists. When they finally returned, Granny didn't know how to tell them. They immediately apologized for staining the floorboards: the movers had broken a five-liter jar of jam.

The Nikiforovs' daughter was married to a Muralov. She hadn't had a church wedding or taken her husband's name because the Socialist-Revolutionary Nikiforovs despised the Social-Democrat Muralovs. Nikolai Ivanovich Muralov later ran the Moscow Military District and supposedly volunteered to kill Stalin. Granny lumped them all together, the Socialist Revolutionaries with the Social Democrats:

"They're all on the lookout for a free meal."

A patriotic display:

Our German teacher to us: "Guten Tag!" We to her: "Zdrastvuite!"

A patriotic act of charity, initiated, no doubt, by the gymnasium:

> A special Russian POSTCARD, name, address.
>
> Written communications to or from prisoners of war are allowed only by means of postcards, openly submitted.
>
> Written communications are allowed only in the Russian, French and German languages.

> An ordinary German POSTKARTE
>
> Postmarked: Kriegsgefangenensendung Gepruft.
> Opened by military censorship, Petrograd.
> Military censor No. 675.

> TO: EVGENIA IVANOVNA NIKITINA
> 8 Bolshaya Kislovka, Apt. 6
> Moscow RUSSIA
> From: Ivan Sidorov Aksyonov
> 1st company of non-commissioned officers
> Prisoner of war camp No. 1
> Altdam Germany

Dear Evgenia Ivanovna, I received your parcel in which I found the items mentioned below, one pair underwear, one towel, socks, tea, sugar, tobacco, soap and biscuits all these are indispensable to me and my heartfelt thanks, but I need comestibles more, and now God bless you and my best wishes non-commissioned officer of the 116th infantry Maloyaroslavsky regiment Ivan Sidorov Aksyonov.

Grandfather was a recruit in a second-class reserve because of his bad health. He wound up in the trenches the second or third year. He soaked and froze in the Carpathians, his head constantly ached.

Granny — a nurse — rushed down to the Carpathians from Moscow. Unable to find Grandfather, she turned in desperation to the Army Commander. Brusilov kissed her hand and asked her to please sit down. Grandfather appeared forthwith — and his conditions improved.

Before being conscripted, he had put money in the bank for Mama and Vera: a thousand rubles each for university. The thousands shriveled up and, one memorable day, disappeared altogether.

Grandfather rejoiced in February of '17: for one thing, he was demobilized; for another, he disliked the tsar — as he did all authorities. At home on Bolshaya Ekaterininskaya he saved the edition of *Russkoye Slovo* with the armed forces' oath of allegiance to the Provisional Government.

Before the Constituent Assembly elections Grandfather worried about how to vote:

"Ignorant fools we are: how should we know? Eh, I'll vote for the Constitutional Democrats, at least they're intelligent..."

From the time the war began, instead of respectable tenants, they had students. Among them Mama's first admirer Tolya Pavperov:

"I was in the seventh grade. And Vera was jealous! She was jealous of all my beaux, made her mad that no one ever called on her. But I didn't like Tolya. I was sly. He'd ask me: 'Zhenia, may I accompany you?' I'd look out the window: if it was rainin', I didn't mind, under an umbrella no one'd see him anyway. He was ugly, face like Socrates'. He and his friends — all students — took me to the Zimin to see *Boris Godunov*. Chaliapin always sang at the Zimin. The Bolshoi was just a name, the Zimin had more seats. They'd put me between'em, then scare the wits out of me sayin' the box-keeper'd come around and ask for my ticket. Couldn't stop shakin'... He was an interestin' person, intelligent. But I wanted someone to dance with, and go skatin'..."

When Pavperov was called up, Gukas, an Armenian, took his place:

"Gukas smelled of burnt skin. People said Armenia was so hot the pigs' skins burst. He went on commissions — in those days everyone went on commissions: gymnasium boys, realists, university students — everyone sympathized with the revolution and kept an eye out for counterrevolutionaries. Mama worried about Gukas, she loved him as if he were her own. She said: 'If my son went on commissions, what would I do? Nothing but pray.' When he came back he said: 'Irina Nikitichna, thank you, you prayed for me...' "

In the fall of '17 Mama worked as a private tutor: there were still places. She prepared the widower Kwalheim's daughters — for what, nobody knows. She went to Professor Bader's daughters as Mademoiselle and taught them French for twenty paper rubles a month. The professor's wife, all done up like a mannequin out of Muir & Merrilees, said things would get even worse. She tried to marry Mama off to a Norwegian, an engineer named Christiansen. Mama was afraid.

"He was sort of an odd one, un-Russian. He'd say: 'Look, I'm wigglin' my ears.' And his ears really did wiggle. I thought to myself: he'll take me away and throw me over. Then what'll I do?"

On Bolshaya Ekaterininskaya someone was the first to say:

"They've been trying to put things right for three hundred years..."

Mama on a camel: a garishly lilac provincial photograph.

After the hungry winter of 1917-18 Granny contracted to work in the quiet and well-fed province of Astrakhan. Her predecessor, doctor's assistant Gogol-Yanovsky (no relation to Father's friend), a general's son, an ignoramus and a do-nothing, hadn't managed. Most likely he couldn't.

"Like Epikhodov, he was a walking disaster."

He had nothing against Granny. He befriended Mama and Vera. His sister Maruska Yanovskaya is — like her brother — a friend of Mama's to this day.

When quiet Akhtuba changed hands, Granny, Yanovsky, Mama and Vera were tending the wounded. Both the Reds and the Whites threatened to hew them down: no one hewed anyone down, they didn't even take prisoners, out of inexperience. Granny favored the ones who were more gentlemanly and a bit more cultivated.

Grandfather couldn't go anywhere: he was immediately recruited to work at the State Depository.

Seated at a refectory table, in identical smocks, faded men are doing some sort of fine work. Grandfather is at the head of the table before an analytical balance, without his moustache, staring straight at the camera. The tormented face of a prisoner. Standing over him is an elephantine overseer.

Compared to his cherished work, the State Depositary was anti-work. The setter had to pick the precious stones out of jewels that had belonged to the court and to the nobility. They brought Grandfather a mangled diadem encrusted with blood and hair: he threw up.

Every morning he changed into a government-issue smock with no pockets, every evening he had to present his anus for inspection:

"As if I were a thief..."

Now it's impossible to understand how the mails went, how they got through the fronts. Granny received a letter saying that Grandfather had Spanish influenza and forced her way through to Moscow! She may have saved him from more than just illness: in his delirium Grandfather kept leaping out of bed in search of a rope:

"But how come I didn't strangle Trotsky..."

In 1920 Mama set off to visit Grandfather and had gone hardly any distance when she was pulled off the train at Saratov with full-blown typhoid:

"Some women carried me to the typhoid barracks. Kept puttin' the stretcher down on the snow to rest. And I kept screamin': 'I'll freeze to death!' I began to get better, the doctor was a nice man, he said: 'If you stay here, in the barracks, you'll pick somethin' else up and you won't get over it.' People've always been kind to me. I wrote to Marusya Yanovskaya's father: if Marusya was in this state, my mama wouldn't leave her to the mercy of fate. He rolled up in a cab, kept urging the horse on, he was afraid I'd freeze to death. When I recovered, I wanted to go to Moscow. But the commissar at the station said: 'Please understand. If I let you go, the first detachment that comes along will pull you off the train and send you to the labor front.' That just made me mad, I didn't understand anything: 'Why'll they pull me off? What labor front?' "

Mama found herself on the Volga at the same time as Papa and also connected to agriculture: for form's sake she had enrolled in a geodetics institute.

It must have been a wonderful time in Saratov: the Volga, freedom, the old blinders gone, the new ones yet to be put on. And s o c i e t y: yesterday's students from Moscow and Petrograd, refugees from western provinces.

"There was this Pole, so sleek and *pshi-vshi*, always bowin' and scrapin'. I, says he, am strong, I'll carry that watermelon for you. But the watermelon was gigantic, he couldn't lift it. He bent down — and broke wind..."

Mama had admirers: h e a p s a n d h e a p s o f ' e m. Even in the wilds of Akhtuba, not counting that lout Yanovsky and officers just passing through, she was seriously courted by the manager of the Baskunchak salt-mines, a fiftyish engineer by the name of Tretyak. He took her for rides in a steam engine and organized picnics on camelback — whence the garishly lilac photograph.

Nothing like that could have happened in Saratov, even without Granny to chaperone: Mama was too much afraid of everything. Besides, she thought of Saratov as a continuation of her gymnasium dances, nothing more. Gatherings by day and by night, strolls, boat trips and songs.

Saratov sufferings — not yet performed by folksy choirs:

> A steamer's sailing down the Volga —
> Oh, Lordy!

Rats are running over the ropes —
Oh, Lordy!

My poor little sweetheart Tanya —
Zhigulechki-Zhiguloo —
Wears a bell about her neck now, —
Look what you've driven her to...

guitars — not yet branded as petty-bourgeois:

I'm a reckless little rogue,
Nothing much matters to me.
If they go and cut my head off,
I'll tie a log on, yessiree!

Ah, I'm in love with just her eyes,
I'm mad about their mischief...

Neapolitan songs — not yet appropriated by the State tenors:

On a breeze light and soft
We'll float high aloft
Wing o'er the ri-ver
Like a bird so quiver.
My little boat is light
My oars are might-ty —
Sa-an-ta-a Lu-u-ci-a,
Santa-a Lucia!

Three dreamy young girls in white dresses, legs dangling over the side of a rowboat. Mama is in the middle, Vera on the right, the year must be 1921, not long before they returned to Moscow.

Grandfather received an award for the State Depositary (it couldn't have been for anything else): a Hero of Labor (*geroi truda*).

Back then it came without any royal insignia or privileges, just a piece of R S F S R e r i z e d letterhead:

"Too rough even to wipe yourself with."

In that era of abbreviations and internationalisms, Grandfather etymologized *geroi truda* the wrong way round:

"The Nikulins have gone queer in the head and made up a name for their little girl: Gertrud."

They informed the Hero of Labor that his jeweler's art was alien to the proletariat and put a knife to his throat: "Join the Party!" At home: "Wife, what should I do, I'd rather hang myself." "You can't join, you'd go out of your mind."

For his refusal, the Hero was stripped of his union work record — he'd been with the metalworkers since 1905.

Incidentally, when the union wouldn't take Mama, she went to *the eater of all those free meals*, the Social Democrat Muralov. The big boss refused to help: "You need to learn to stand up for yourself." That sounded like a line out of the famous Socialist Revolutionary song: *In the struggle your rights you shall find.*

Grandfather worked at Schwalbe (fine medical instruments) and Granny at Sklifosovsky Hospital. They scraped by. Grandfather was indignant: "Some get paid, others don't. Even so they pay a pittance, and today they were collecting for the English miners again. They're on strike! But they live a thousand times better than us. And they're not stuck with any Yid-plan..."

Promfinplan (the industrial-financial plan), given the domination of the Yids, had become Yid-plan.

In 1921 Mama entered the natural sciences department of Moscow University I, couldn't bear the dissecting room and switched to chemistry.

At the very first lecture she glanced round the auditorium and remarked to the girl sitting next to her:

"Nothin' but Jews!"

The girl was also Jewish.

Mama was hauled up before every committee.

"Are you the daughter of the furrier Mikhailov?"

As in the popular ditty:

> I'm not farm and I'm not state,
> Nor a union member, oh dear,
> If they decide to check,
> I'll be out on my ear.

They decided to check. They asked Mama: "What's the difference between the Party and the government."

Mama thought a minute: "There isn't any."

They laughed. They didn't see the insult to their party's majesty.

Oh, how one wanted to insult them. Granny picked this up at Sklifosovsky:

> The tsar bell doesn't ring,
> The tsar cannon doesn't shoot,
> The chervonets buys nothing,
> And now Lenin is mute.

> Amidst horns a-droning,
> Amidst Yids a-moaning,
> We bid farewell to our Messiah,
> And ever grateful Mother Russia
> Whilst cannons and mortars screamed
> Hustled him off to the latrine.

Once a friend of Mama's, in her cups, sang for all to hear:

> I'll buy a candle, I will,
> Til-lill, til-lill tra-la,
> For Lenin's grave, I will
> Ho-ho! Ha-ha!
> It'll burn as bright as brass,
> Til-lill, til-lill tra-la,
> In Lenin's bright red ass,
> Ho-ho! Ha-ha!

She sang out and was sent up. When she came back, people were afraid of her: somehow it had been impressed upon them that to come back from there was unnatural. Pointing at the big building on the corner of Solyanka:

"They shoot them in the cellars there — then dump the bodies in the Moscow River."

"They say Savinkov was a bag of bones when they threw him in."

People figured out who the d i r t y r a t s were; but they never let the rats know they knew — because you never know...

As for the n o t h i n ' b u t J e w s, Mama's admirers from the university were Russian:

Dmitry Yazykov, a medical student:

> Dmitry of the Don, I'm not,
> Not the False Dmitry either,
> But plain old Dmitry, that sot,
> That champion imbiber.

Gavka Popov, also a medical student. His father had owned a big timber-rafting business. Gavka concealed the fact but was found

11*

out because of sending packages up North. He died in a prison lumber camp.

Kolya Saburov, a secret nobleman and rising chemistry star, survived.

Kolya Shuikin, also a chemistry student. He wrote Mama poems in the manner of Esenin.

They were as plentiful as fish in the sea, who could remember them all?

And every one of them had his own Bolshaya Ekaterininskaya — in Moscow or in the provinces. Every one, like Mama, would have been accepted to the university even without the *Revolushit*. Every one felt compelled to rush in with flowers:

> A rose will wilt in the frost,
> But not your beauty ne'er lost.

And every one was nonplussed by the mandatory Marxism course. If they were alienated in a class sense, they were not at all hostile. They were not one of them and did not aspire to be, but by now they were being swept along by the tide and only God could save them, lost souls, from what to them would be an unfathomable end.

Oh, the songs they sang!

A city chastushka:

> Was it you who wasted me or I you
> Was it you who ruined me or I you?
> Was it you who splashed me with the jug or I you?
> Was it you who splashed me with the pail or I you?

The same thing with a certain *je ne sais quoi*:

> The singer's lovely aria ria-ria,
> We had the luck to hear it oh-oh:

They drenched him, Santa Maria ria-ria-ria,
With something from the window-ow-ow.
Awash in tears a living soul-oul-oul
Oh, that cursed Belvedere-dere-dere!
And smashing his new bass viol-ol-ol
The officer did disappear-pear-pear.

Heroic-prewar:

If girl-students flew through the air,
Then boy-students would become aviators
From dawn, from dawn and again till dawn,
From dusk, from dusk and again till dawn.

Vampuka:

We're E, we're thi, we're o, we're pians,
We're E-thi-o-pians.
Oppon-oppon, oppon-oppon,
Opponents of Europeans.
In black Af, in black Af,
In black Africa we live.
Vampu-Vampu, Vampu-Vampu,
Vampuka we will find:
Hip-hip-hooray, hip-hip-hooray,
Hip-hip-hooray, hooray, hooray...

NEP-era:

But he hadn't loved Klava long,
Before the sad end came along:
The prole was caught stealing,
The Cheka sent him reeling,
Right into the slammer clang-bang, ding-dong.

He sat down and sadly stared,
Wishing his Klava were there...

Chemistry department:

Karl Ivanich with the long nose
Came with a question to me:
"What can I do with my long nose?"
"Rub it with vitriol, you'll see!
Just take some alum, like this,
Now in the alum go and piss,
Let it stand out in the snow:
And you'll have vitriol, just so."

Homespun:

These times they are incredible,
Not a day goes by but a miracle:
Now they distil alcohol from shit,
Just a quarter of a pood, that's it.
The inventive Russian mind does know
How to please the European masses:
Soon alcohol will flow
Into mouths straight from asses.

Unlike Mama's beaux, Granny and Grandfather were not lost souls. Silently, without a word and without demur, they counted themselves among the vanquished. Aloud they raged and reminisced about life in p e a c e t i m e:

"Then, too, we lived on buckwheat, but no one hauled you in."

In the *Moscow Jeweler's Association*, and later in the *Photo-jeweler* artel, they paid little and suspected much. They shook Grandfather down routinely, demanded gold and diamonds. They held him in the Lubyanka sweatbox more than once. And regaled him with tales of this gadget: they insert it in your anus and then there's nothing you won't give them.

Grandfather was ready to give them everything down to the last wedding ring. But Granny wouldn't let him. She knew better: the more you give them, the less likely they are to leave you alone. Thanks to her fury a few things were kept back.

Coupled with this pragmatic fury was a naive precaution. Next to the round turn-bell by the door to their apartment on Bolshaya Ekaterininskaya, a sign said PLEASE TURN: this was for strangers (from the GPU?). Family and friends knew to tap on the wall with a key.

During practical training, Mr. Ralle, a concessionaire, presented Mama with his masterpiece, *Bilitis* perfume: a gold-tinted brass box with a bas-relief of an invented Greek poetess, and inside, between little silk pillows, a phial with a gold-tinted metal label, Bilitis in all her pulchritude.

After university — beginning in 1927 — Mama worked at a factory, Red Soap, belonging to Zhirkost Trust. The factory was at the end of the earth and stank to high heaven.

Her job consisted of quality checks, like assignments she had been given in gymnasium.

"They felt sorry for me, I never worked the night shift, I was delicate..."

They felt sorry for her and took her into the trade union, they felt sorry for her and gave her easy volunteer work: distributing theater tickets allotted to the factory. The proletariat said: "Give us light opera. We don't need *The Lower Depths*, we see that every day."

Zhirkost Trust. Its emblem was a T growing up over the Zh.

The head of the laboratory, another of Mama's admirers, was always assuring her: "Who are we? Zh/T: Zhenia and Tolya. But Tolya will get the upper hand."

Neither our erstwhile tenant Tolya Pavperov, Mama's first beau, nor Tolya-the-head-of-the-lab, got the upper hand.

Mama's first husband was an engineer by the name of Kamandin. About him I know that he was not very tall, well-proportioned, and wore, according to the fashion then, a pince-nez and close-cropped hair.

"He was so hard and callous. You think he'd've let me finish university? I went to Bolshaya Ekaterininskaya and said: 'Take me back!' I just ran away, fled in a carrier's cart, leavin' all my things behind. My German books, my readers. I only sent Nadka Pavlova round to him for my skates: what was I to do without skates?"

Come to think of it, she was lucky she ran away: a few years later Kamandin fell in with the Industrial Party.

"Everyone said then that it wasn't them at the trial, but folks in disguise. I just don' know, I was so upset, I turned black from worry."

I don't think Mama was ever hauled in. The thought of her in Lubyanka with an investigator is frightening.

"When the doctor saw my hemoglobin was 57 percent, she wrote a note straightaway to the head of production, said I needed a vacation. The factory got me a student voucher for the Black Sea, for Sudak. I looked young, no one guessed I was thirty. I didn't have any money to pay for the trip so I went to the head of production and said: 'Give me a month's advance and I'll work it off when I get back.' He smiled: 'Zhenia, you can't do that. Here's a bonus, don't you tell anyone.' They had bonuses and I didn't even know it... So I went off and had a rest, got my strength back at least."

She warmed herself in the sun: in the photographs she is, in fact, remarkably young and pretty. She took walks along the shore: she couldn't swim and in the mountains she was afraid of heights.

Sudak was Mama's last trip:

Mama never was in Leningrad,
Mama never was in Kiev,
never cared about anything,
never made any effort whatsoever,
never seriously thought about anything,
never acknowledged the exalted and the absolute,
never believed in God,
never thought of anyone as her equal,
never was unhappy with herself,
never doubted that she was right,
never was able to put herself in someone else's shoes,
never kept cats or dogs or flowers,
never fell in love,
never believed anyone except Granny,
never identified herself with the regime,
never betrayed anyone.

Mama's sister Vera had begun to stray from Bolshaya Ekaterininskaya. She had been accepted to the Moscow Art Institute and was studying under Mashkov and Konchalovsky. Sokolov-Skalya gave her the willies. She adored contemporary Western painting and literature:

"Two or three strokes and you see everything."

In a small whitewashed cupboard behind glass:

    Pushkin in Life

    Yezhov and Shamurin

    Rose and Cross

    Russian Futurism

    Gypsy Stories (Berkovich)

    A Strange Occurrence in Western City

    A New Southern Discovery or the French Daedalus

And pamphlets: Tretyakov Art Gallery, Museum of New Western Art, Cezanne, Steinlen, Masereel, Kathe Kollwitz, A Stroll through the Trans-Baltic, Child Artists. And a Persimfans concert program.

In the revolutionary art journal *Art for the Masses*, I came across an improbable letter to the editor from a certain "s e l f - t a u g h t   T o c h i l k i n" and some devastating verses in the manner of Demyan Bedny:

> I went to watch the October parade on Red Square,
> And just opposite the Kremlin there stared,
> The image of a Red soldier
> On a huge gray canvas.
> A lumbering dunderhead doubled poster-wise
> And frankly freakish at twice the size.
> On another poster, the proletariat,
> That boxy freak, flaunted its ugly mug.
> Voroshilov exploded: "Is this a blunder or a slight?
> Take those abominations out of my sight!
> A wanton act of sabotage seems to me..."

Books, pamphlets and even jaunty verses were in the front. Below, behind tightly closed doors, lay means beyond description:

    burnt sienna,

    raw umber,

Prussian blue,
emerald green,
cobalt blue,
chrome yellow,
Mars brown,
cadmium red,
ultramarine,
caput mortuum,
madder lake,
gamboge...

Real paints — German, English — had long since disappeared, as had the best Russian ones. Canvases, too, were not to be had. Vera painted three or four pictures — layer upon layer — on one. Mama often posed: a life model free of charge. Vera's classmate painted her all dressed up and decked out; Vera put her in a peasant dress with vegetables. Vera always started off well, but didn't know when to stop, she tortured her canvases to gloom.

Gloomy: that, if you like, is the word for Vera.

She had aristocratic looks, like Grandfather. But she was wildly temperamental, and eccentric, more so than Grandfather. She despised men — especially Mama's beaux. *Vera's swain hadn't been born yet.*

If she hadn't been pregnant with me, Mama would hardly have married Father? Or perhaps the other way round? Perhaps she had no choice but to become pregnant with me so that Father would marry her? The dates of her marriage and my birth are awfully close. Mama's words:

"Friends said they'd introduce me to a cattle-feeder. A lot of girls were after him to marry them. But I wouldn't take no for an answer... He couldn't make up his mind. Told me I was frivolous. And it's true, I never did stop to think if I was doin' the right thing or not..."

Father couldn't make up his mind for good reason: he'd just been married.

At forty, in '30, he had married the sister of Nadka Pavlova, Mama's old school friend. She quickly and publicly began an affair with a mutual acquaintance. Father walked out. Mama l a t c h e d o n t o   h i m then went quick to the recent wife to find out what sort of a person Yakov was and generally...

Just as no one at Bolshaya Ekaterininskaya was glad of my Father, so everyone was glad of me. Granny never left us, in Moscow or in Udelnaya. Every day in Moscow either we went to her or she came to us, especially in the morning, after Sklifosovsky where she was o n f o r t w e n t y - f o u r h o u r s t h e n o f f f o r f o r t y- e i g h t. She worked in surgery with Professor Yudin.

Yudin said: "I'm not running a nursing home!"

When internal passports were introduced, Granny shaved eight years off her age against the future.

Grandfather never once came to Kapelsky Lane, let alone to Udelnaya.

Father appeared at Bolshaya Ekaterininskaya perforce. He sat at the table and either said nothing or remarked on the wooden breadbasket with its archaic inscription: HEARTY APPETITE! In Usolye there had been one even better: BREAD AT TABLE — HANDS ABLE!

Mama preferred thin slices — l i k e p e t a l s. Grandfather cut hunks:

"A big piece gladdens the mouth!"

Mostly at Bolshaya Ekaterininskaya they ate:

"Cabbage soup and kasha: our daily ration."

On paydays Grandfather l i v e d i t u p : he fried potatoes, thick slabs, in lots of clarified butter. I liked them more than Granny's delicacies from Eliseyev's. Grandfather beamed:

"Our farmer boy!"

When I dropped food on the floor, he gave countenance:

"No Russian will eat what hasn't lain around."

When I fussed or demanded, he approved:

"Our hero! Give it to him at all costs!"

Granny was jealous because *I took entirely after Grandfather.* Mama explained: "He was born on Spirits' Day so he's spirited." Vera didn't reason: "My deary duck."

And from then on, as far back as I can remember, I was showered with all manner of folklore: ancient and post-Revolutionary, village and urban, popular and homespun, frank and affected.

The broadcasts we heard on Kapelsky were the same ones everyone heard everywhere. Except on Bolshaya Ekaterininskaya: Granny and Grandfather had no loudspeaker, and they weren't the only ones.

In 1937 Mama's first husband, the exile Kamandin, turned up in Moscow — by some miracle, for one day — all the way from Kara-Bogaz. He came to Kapelsky in the afternoon when Papa was at Timiryazev. He begged Mama to come away with him and offered to adopt me. Mama soberly refused. Stunned, I reported to Papa that evening:

"There was a man here, he drank vodka and cried on the pickles."

Everyone was being imprisoned. Granny and Grandfather, naturally, didn't for one minute believe that any of the people arrested were guilty. They weren't worried for themselves:

"There's no escaping fate. And if it's not our fate, then nothing will happen."

They trembled for their family and friends and were indignant for others. Grandfather was not indignant over the show trials:

"Why should I feel sorry for Bukharin? I feel sorry for Nikulin." (Nikulin was a neighbor and colleague.)

Lion Feuchtwanger rode about Moscow like royalty, accompanied by his translator, the younger Trubnikova. He even visited his translator's simple abode: the Trubnikovs and the Balandins had bought the cooperative apartment that had belonged to the famous surgeon Burdenko for the handsome sum of fourteen thousand rubles. It was at a New Year's party there that everything had seemed so incomprehensibly beautiful to me and, as at the dacha, roomy.

The translator whispered into Granny's ear how much she had seen them pay Feuchtwanger for his *Moscow, 1937* and how much they had offered him to stay on.

In the communal kitchen on Kapelsky Lane Mama would announce loudly, just in case:

"That Gaidar has a good face."

"I sobbed and sobbed over *How the Steel Was Tempered*: it was just so movin'."

"Just full of feelin'!" — about Chkalov's favorite song:

Singing songs, fighting and triumphant,
Our people will always follow Stalin.

Either because of her nasty nature, or perhaps because of her Cezannism, after a successful opening in '37, Vera's pictures vanished from the exhibition hall. They were found in a dark closet.

Vera stayed in her room for several days. Then suddenly, petitions in hand, she rushed off to find Defense Commissar Voroshilov and commissars even higher up. Her parents' views and her own notwithstanding, Vera believed men in uniform.

Once when I was at Bolshaya Ekaterininskya, a doctor arrived in an NKVD uniform. Vera refused to talk to him. She said it wasn't a real NKVD uniform and the man was a Jew.

It truly wasn't a real uniform, she insisted. Jews were the root of all evil:

Jews were disembowelers. They deformed our skulls by night, scooped out our bones and broke them, sawed off bits of our teeth, and changed the color of our eyes and hair with injections so there wouldn't be any Russians with blue eyes and blond hair.

Jews were r i t u a l i s t s. They surrounded us with their words, their words were everywhere, in assonances and accent shifts.

Jews were S c h u t z b u n d n i k s. Day and night they stifled our thoughts with their r a c k e t, or read our thoughts with a r h e o s t a t, a rheostat was a t h i n k e r.

Vera also said that, as a precaution, one should get rid of all markings, symbols and insignia. She scrubbed *SAZIKOV* and *84* off the spoons, *SOLINGEN* and the little sheep off the knives and scissors, *POPOV* off the sewing machine, *No. 4711* off the face powder, and the *SIU* off the fruit-drop tins. Using half a draftsman's razor blade broken on the diagonal, she picked out her birthmarks and freckles.

Complete salvation was to be had in the book *Baghdad* with its preface by Dzhugashvili. But the book was hard to find, and even if you did find it, the preface would have been torn out (all prefaces were torn out then).

Only free tillers of the soil were safe from Jews: Granny's family from Ozherelye, say, except their rights had been revoked. *Citizen*, as a form of address, protected one. Vera would say to me:

"Citizen's home."

"Citizen, would you like some grated carrot?"

Anyone could turn out to be a Jew:

"I woke up in the night and saw old woman Rizhova coming down from the ceiling."

Old woman Rizhova was Granny's sister, my Great Aunt Asya, Rizhova by marriage. A kinder, meeker, more considerate and affectionate person you couldn't imagine. I loved her the best of all my relations — and not even because she always brought me something that Boris and Igor had grown out of:

another set of *Hedgehog*, the children's magazine,

tiddlywinks,

a crude album with stamps: "This is just to start the ball rolling."

I tried to picture the album starting my ball rolling.

Instead of the usual kopeck, she always put a ten-kopeck piece in my money-box: "You'll be better off with silver." I pictured mountains of silver. Her poor presents were always rich.

Great Aunt Asya never raised her voice. With affection and gentle hints she coaxed slow-on-the-uptake me into wanting/doing what I should and behaving as I ought.

The Ryzhovs lived in half a shack in Pokrovskoe-Glebovo, then outside Moscow. Great Aunt Asya's husband, the Chekhovian bore Dmitry Petrovich, joked about it:

"Saint Glebeau."

Their sons Boris and Igor sat by the roadside for days on end and jotted down the numbers of passing cars: were any of them the same? Had anyone noticed them doing this, they would have been convicted of e s p i o n a g e.

Papa earned more than Granny and Grandfather put together; Dmitry Petrovich and Great Aunt Asya earned less. For lack of means their sons went into the military. The younger one, Igor, was kept from the front by a rare tropical disease. The older one, handsome Boris, t h e v e r y b e s t o f h i s m o t h e r a n d f a t h e r, exploded in air over his own aerodrome. Great Aunt Asya journeyed to his grave *near Smolensk*. If not for eyewitnesses, she could have hoped that Boris was somewhere among the former prisoners of war, dispersed like the Jews.

In 1937 or '38, Great Uncle Semyon, the Gypsy, the man of affairs, Granny's brother and Mama's godfather, sneaked back to Moscow from his place of exile in Voronezh.

It is no accident that the entrepreneur in Erdman's *The Suicide* was one Kalabushkin, owner of a shooting gallery in the *Proletarian Beaumonde Garden*. My Great Uncle Semyon, Semyon Nikitich Kalabushkin, leased that same *Yar* — with gypsies — in Petrovsky Park. He also owned a restaurant — first at Petrovskiye Vorota and then on Bolshaya Dmitrovskaya Street — where he tried to fatten up that seedy idol, the singer Damaev. Mama would occasionally stop by on her way home from university:

"Made your mouth water!"

But when she was completely out-of-pocket or once, when she'd lost the housekeeping money, the godfather would loan his goddaughter money at interest. Even so, his wife, Great Aunt Varya, disapproved:

"Kalabushkin is a duffer, he'll leave his children beggars..."

It wasn't he who left them beggars.

Great Aunt Varya lived near Nikitskiye Vorota in a 10-square-meter room with her family of four: herself, her daughter Margushka, her grandson Andrei, and her son-in-law Kimryakov.

Kimryakov praised his absent father-in-law:

"I take my hat off to Semyon Nikitich: a simple shepherd — and look how he moved up in the world!"

At some point two young poets arrived from the provinces to try and win Moscow. Sergei Mikhalkov made a lasting marriage to the daughter of Konchalovsky (granddaughter of Surikov, the painter). His friend Volodya Kimryakov, if he's to be believed, was first married to Lyubov Orlova. Then he latched onto Margushka — possibly for the sake of Great Uncle Semyon's fortune. So far as literature is concerned, the poet Mikhalkov received a medal, while the poet Kimryakov had one fable published in *Ogonyok* — *Two Hedgehogs and Two Ruffs* — which Mama always sneered at.

Kimryakov was somehow thought to be an informer. Perhaps for this reason, or perhaps for some other, Great Aunt Varya wouldn't let her exiled husband in.

Even Semyon's son Volodka — the engineer and future collector of Chinese antiquities, who had already been to Italy — was afraid. Volodka's wife, the children's poetess Olga Gurian, threw her father-in-law out on his ear and bellowed after him down the stairwell:

"If you ever show your face here again, I'll tell the house committee to have you arrested..."

Bolshaya Ekaterininskaya was off-limits because of Vera's illness.

In Pokrovskoe-Glebovo he begged Great Aunt Asya:

"Dig a hole in the yard. I'll give you lots of money."

Great Aunt Asya was afraid: for her children and especially for Dmitry Petrovich, an honest man, but a coward and dangerously naive.

Great Uncle Semyon turned up at his goddaughter's — in Udelnaya, that is — in tears. I don't remember his face, but I do remember how naturally he pulled out a pocketknife, cut a hazel branch and whittled me a green shepherd's pipe in ten minutes.

He didn't ask to dig a hole in our yard: either he was on his guard with my father, who wouldn't have refused, or he had already found a place.

On the way back to Voronezh he bandaged his gold and diamonds to his leg. They arrested him at the station.

Great Aunt Katya, Granny's older sister, the feeble-minded one, was invariably herself. When she saw the piano in our cramped Kapelsky quarters:

"Where'd you put the Pioneer?"

And for all Udelnaya to hear:

"It was that Trotskin, the Yids and the styudents that made the Revolyutchion!"

Her daughter Maria, a Party member, agreed with her most likely — just as in the summer of '17 she had agreed with any public speaker: she liked them all. Maria took after her mother and never learned anything. On the other hand, she was the only one in the family to join the Party voluntarily and she earned more than my

Papa the associate professor: she checked winning bonds at the State Bank and — she made no secret of the fact — informed. There were those who pressed Maria to tell them how the State swindled them with loans — but she guarded the secret devoutly. When she took me for walks, she told me stories of the bourgeois dragging our comrades away on the border and torturing them.

Great Aunt Katya's son Sergei was older than Maria. When Mama played lord-and-lady with him, Maria was the maid.

Sergei had gone out into the world when still a boy and acquired a colorful resume. He had been a printer's apprentice, had secretly printed something for the Social Democrats and been imprisoned, supposedly by Malinovsky himself. After the *Revolushit*, he had worked for the Cheka and begun to go out of his mind:

"We caught a young fellow on a bicycle and stood him up against the wall: he was a spy. He said: 'Let me pray to God', and got down on his knees. We beat him to death. I feel badly for him, can't get him out of my mind, see him in my dreams. I told the doctor: 'You see, I hear little birds singing in my head,' and walked out."

It was at this point in his life and work that he married the Baroness von Morgenshtierna: he carried her off from a Baltic German castle and received for dowry a disfranchised mother-in-law.

Around the same time he was expelled from the Party. He lived in Kiev for twenty years and, in the opinion of his Moscow relations, became completely Y i d d i f i e d.

He would sit in the rocking chair on our veranda in Udelnaya merrily telling stories about Jews:

"An Indian delegate was late for the Comintern Congress. Dispatches were sent out to every station. From Zhmerinka came the reply: 'Rabinowitz is painting himself red, he'll be on his way as soon as he dries.'"

"My friend Sheferson had his half-belt cut off on the tram. As we were getting off the tram, I noticed he had a half-belt in his hands. 'What, you found it?' 'No, I cut another one off just like mine!'"

"Old man Sheferson was complaining to me about life. I said: 'What can you do? *Lioshioskho kevisi adenoi.*' He took my Iosif aside: 'That a Jew?' 'No, a goy.' 'Then that's a highly educated man, he knows Hebrew...'"

As corroboration Sergei left me Shalom Aleichem's *Notes of a Commercial Traveler.*

I asked him to bring me my beloved *Gavroche* from Moscow.

"I read your *Gavroche* on the train with great pleasure."

Sergei's pronunciation grated slightly. And yet his ebullience, brilliance, and breadth enchanted me. I even regretted aloud that he wasn't my father.

My father often kidded Sergei:

"You do talk a lot of hot air..."

Sergei, too, became attached to me, gave me presents and spent time with me. With him I easily parried the most involved jokes, was smooth and witty myself, flimflammed him at cards and boasted to him about my *enviable things* in the brass Bilitis perfume box. Sergei nicknamed me O s t a p B e n d e r. I knew it was a good word.

Once, when we were at the table at Bolshaya Ekaterininskaya, he said:

"Our country's only concern for people is that they kick the bucket faster."

He wasn't joking. Now it seems to me that he even opposed the actual situation.

I heard about the care he took of his wife and daughter. When they wound up on occupied territory, he transferred that caring to us: he constantly sent remittances to his mother (Great Aunt Katya), to my granny, to Mama. To me — specially — he wired 150 rubles. Later he sent a parcel: rolled sheets of whatman paper covered with Soviet stamps rifled from a local history museum during the Soviet retreat. I wrote to him on a handmade postcard bought at the bazaar — all stenciled pansies:

> Dear Uncle Sergei,
>
> How are you? I am already in second grade. Thank you very much for the 3 posters. I received them on the 19th of July. I am living at the dacha. Granny says to thank you for the money. We are all alive so far, but I am often sick.
>
> Much love,
>
> 19/X '42 Andrei

The letter was never sent: just as the Stalingrad campaign was beginning Sergei announced himself at Bolshaya Ekaterininskaya. He had been putting up fortifications outside Stalingrad when the Germans came up from the wrong side. The little birds began singing in his head again and he received a permanent exemption.

He explained what happened:

"The war started because Hitler realized that the bandit had it in for him. So he attacked. Otherwise we would have attacked in '42..."

He was staying with his sister when an old acquaintance from the Cheka suddenly appeared at the door: he had seen Sergei somewhere and followed him home. Sergei pretended not to know him, pretended that it was some mistake, that he was not he, and then he spent many, many nights at my granny's.

He gave me everything of his that was remarkable except his Canadian root pipe, and when I coveted that, he stopped me:

"Andrei, that's aggression."

He took me to the circus and to the movies — *George from Dinky Jazz*, *The Three Musketeers*. He told me that war was not an adventure but a way of life, that the Germans dressed elegantly and that their iron-cross made a somber and majestic impression.

I complained that there was almost nothing beautiful around me and pointed to the wretched little houses along Bolshaya Ekaterininskaya.

"Come now! Give every house an owner, fix it up, touch it up, and there would be such beauty you couldn't tear your eyes away."

Sergei found work on the labor front near Moscow: he ran a lumber works where he surrounded himself with an entire harem. His favorite of favorites, a d i v i n e d o c t o r — Sergei had drunk vodka with her pilot husband — gave me a P u s h k i n r u b l e , a ruble from 1836.

Sergei listed Vera, who had run away from the clinic, as a member of his staff so that she could have a worker's ration card: she couldn't actually work. So that Mama could have a worker's ration card and so she wouldn't wind up on the labor front, Margushka's husband Kimryakov gave her a job in the Industrial Artist artel. Seamstresses working at home sewed repulsive little Eskimo dolls. Mama kept the card, the money went to Kimryakov.

Loving us and surrounded by his harem, Sergei longed desperately for his wife, the Baronessa von Morgenshtierna, and his daughter Margarita. He knew for certain that they were in Kiev. He kept hoping they would be evacuated, kept making inquiries.

It was only after the liberation of Kiev — and even then not right away — that a letter arrived from a neighbor: yes, they had stayed. Eighteen-year-old Margarita had died in the summer of '41, evidently while digging trenches. His wife, because of hunger and at his mother-in-law's insistence, had declared herself *Volksdeutsche* (of German origin). No one knew this word in Moscow. Her handwriting was hard to read. Mama misread the word as *Volksfeind* (enemy of the people) and decided it was in German so that it would get through *checked by military censorship*.

Journal:

8 February 1944

Tuesday. On Sunday Sergei went with me to the stamp store and bought me 24 stamps for 80 rubles... On Saturday Sergei came to see us, he can't get permission to go to Kiev...

9 June 1944

Sergei sent a letter from Kiev not long ago: Margarita and Olga Romanovna are dead.

Many years after the war the Baroness wrote Sergei from Poland. She had retreated with the Germans as far as Poznan where she had married an elderly Pole:

"He is like a father to me..."

Every winter of the war, *so we wouldn't kick the bucket*, swollen purple Great Aunt Fenia, the *Kalabushkin family beauty*, made the journey to Moscow from Ozherelye with a pood of honey for all her sisters. The honey was divided equally, in the end it wasn't that much. Grandfather and Papa gave their shares to us. Granny tried to fatten up Vera, t h e p o o r t h i n g, and Mama because she was d e l i c a t e, and especially m e. She always forgot about herself, and no one reminded her. Meanwhile, during those hungry years, I learned to distinguish different kinds and hues of honey.

Great Aunt Fenia had had a weak heart from childhood, had remained in the country and happily married an educated peasant, Ivan Pavlovich Bychkov. He was a huge reader, a jack-of-all-trades and an icon-dauber. He painted cupids on the ceilings of Great Uncle Semyon's restaurants. He was the first one in Ozherelye to have an apiary. My granny took out a subscription to a bee-keeping magazine for him.

During collectivization, envious neighbors, aided by Bychkov's own Komsomol son, concocted a denunciation against him: he owned not 6, but 600 dessiatines of land. Ivan Pavlovich was not dispossessed but arrested. Two or three years later the only letter arrived — some kind person had mailed it — from Karaganda. The gist: don't wait.

The apiary outlived its master, and ailing, country-poor Great Aunt Fenia gave the honey to us city folk. And the letters she wrote! According to all the rules: *To begin with...* and she would list to whom and in what order her respects should be given. And so full of life: she wrote the way she spoke, phonetic transcriptions of accounts of the news in Ozherelye, of her son and daughter-in-law's latest skullduggery...

The winter of '42-'43, Mama and I lived at Granny's: the central heating wasn't working, somehow or other we managed to fire the Dutch stove.

In Vera's rocking chair I read a pre-revolutionary edition of *Arabian Nights*, searched for *Barsak's Expedition* in sets of *Pioneer* magazine, and shunned *The Great Opposition* and *Old Man Khottabych. Wild Dog Dingo* nipped sweetly, *A Military Secret* scared me, *The School in the Forest* awakened kind feelings.

With Granny I took to going around the neighborhood. On Bolshaya Ekaterininskaya and on Malaya Ekaterininskaya I saw antique vases, carpets, statuettes and icon-cases with enameled images of Saint Seraphim of Sarov. In one place I was given an Easter postcard, in another a tsarist stamp, in still another a Napoleon III franc. Once Granny, exulting, brought me a thick rough copper coin with two figures and a capital M on it:

"Could be Tsar Mikhail Fyodorovich!"

Great Aunt Varya — wife of the vanished Gypsy, Great Uncle Semyon — got under my skin:

"I once had a copper coin with Christ on it, Byzantine."

To comfort me, Granny secretly gave me a brand new 1818 five-ruble note.

After the small silver coins, Grandfather presented me with a Soviet ruble with a worker and a peasant on it:

"There used to be a *chervonets*: it looked like a tsarist 10-ruble note, only with a peasant sowing grain."

To him I was no longer a farmer boy, but a rag-and-bone man.

Grandfather tried to take me to the *Express* cinema — out of habit he still called it the *Invalides* — to see *Peter the Great*. They didn't let me in because I was *under sixteen*.

"*Peter the Great* was a good picture. So was *Chapayev*. I liked the psychological attack. I saw that movie four times because of it."

(Papa remembered something different from *Chapayev*: *You are sleeping, phantom heroes...*)

Grandfather taught me to play chess. His chessmen were revolutionary: the usual pieces, only not black and white, but black and red — so that no one would be white. On the board, a small plate covered one square:

> "To comrade I.M. Mikhailov from the Photo-Jeweler chess collective, which took 2nd place in the 1st tournament 10/VII-'33."

Papa I sometimes beat, Grandfather never once.

Papa came by almost every evening. He brought potatoes, went to the pump for water, chopped wood and carried it in from the shed, ate *ratatouille soup* with everyone else and talked guardedly of the war and politics.

On Sundays he took me for walks. Once when he was in the outhouse — the plumbing in the house had frozen — someone outside whacked him on his bare behind with a stick. Papa laughed when he told the story.

I had gone off skiing by myself — there were no other children in 5a — and was suddenly surrounded by *Timur and His Team*. They tried to snatch one of my ski poles. I was so outraged, I didn't scream: I stood my ground and fought back. They took the pole and disappeared. I didn't laugh when I told the story. I tried to stay indoors.

I was always being chased outside to take walks with Vera. I listened to her rant about the Jews for hours on end, and nodded in abominable agreement: Vera gave me stamps — Hungarian ones with the parliament and reapers; colonial ones with natives and landscapes; Greek ones with vases and sculptures. She glued her stamps firmly into a little album and etched their serrated edges with gold paint:

"That's the fashion now abroad."

Certain stamps she burned after showing them to me. She burned all her canvases and sketches then started on her books. No one tried to stop her:

"They're her things. She does what she wants with them."

Only Papa officially bought *Pushkin in Life* from her. A boxed *Academia* edition.

Vera had become a chronic invalid, confined to the Belye Stolby

Clinic. Granny went out to see her twice a month on the rare, almost unscheduled, local steam-train — a w h o l e r i g m a r o l e. Mama went out once then w a s l a i d u p for three days.

Vera was always demanding to be taken home, and pitching out the food visitors had managed to scrape together.

She often ran away. Once home, she would slap Granny across the face; Grandfather she was afraid of. She would recount incarceration horrors — most likely the honest truth.

Orderlies from Stolby would barge in after her and take her back — sometimes by force. Other times Granny couldn't stand it: she would keep Vera after signing for her and endure the consequences.

Journal:

17 July 1944
Vera has gone completely crazy: when Igor arrived she called him a Schutzbundnik and spat in his face.

She spat at Great Aunt Asya and at Papa. Papa made light of it: "Shortfall, Vera Ivanovna."

She made ridiculous faces back at him and stuck out her tongue.

In some strange way, Papa respected Vera. He valued her cultivation and her artistic nature. Before the war, when she was better, he found her work doing diagrams for Timiryazev for which he took full responsibility.

Vera still loved me and paid me all kinds of attention. To me her presence was increasingly unbearable. She would sit there saying nothing and make me want to run far, far away. Papa tried to protect me, he would protest or say something to Vera in a friendly way. Meanwhile, Grandfather, o u r v e r y o w n t y r a n t, worried that Vera would murder us all in our beds. In vain. Granny's pity for her unfortunate daughter always won out.

Granny went on working at Sklifosovsky Hospital, only now she was in the emergency ward — t w e n t y - f o u r h o u r s o n t h e n f o r t y - e i g h t o f f. Her month's pay together with her pension was enough for three or four market-bought loaves of bread or five or six kilos of potatoes. But then she supplied all her relations with medicine — even sulfapyridine. That she might sell these medicines never occurred to her. Granny loved to physic people.

She physicked us at home — too much, perhaps. And she physicked her colleagues at work.

According to one story she gave Professor Yudin xeroformium powder for his dysentery — and it cured him for good.

Her own illnesses went untreated: *nothing bothers me*. When her appendix became inflamed she refused to be operated on.

Work in the emergency ward was backbreaking, and the things one saw made life seem even more terrible than it was:

A child swallowed a safety-razor blade.

Workers got blind drunk on methyl alcohol.

A pane of glass fell edgewise on a pedestrian from an upper story.

Thieves pumped a cop full of air with an automobile pump inserted in his anus.

In the middle of a shift, Granny came rushing home — just to make sure. They'd brought in a little boy who'd been run over by a trolleybus: he looked just like me.

Granny took care of Mama until the last: perhaps she knew Mama wouldn't be able to manage on her own. Mama *never made any effort whatsoever* — and when I was born no small effort was required. Mama was exhausted and constantly i n d i s p o s e d. Someone said the word: hypertension. And the word caught on.

"I'm hypertensive!"

"You think I'm a person? I'm half a person..."

First thing in the morning, her head swathed in a wet towel:

"Ah, my head, my head, might as well be dead..."

It fell to Granny to teach me good sense. She explained history and politics to me and overthrew idols:

"Moustached sadist!" (About Stalin.)

"Someone asks Lenin: 'Vladimir Ilyich, why is your hand always in your pocket?' 'I'm getting up a Communist cell: a member and two sympathizers.'"

Granny didn't allow me to take the Lord's name in vain when I had read my fill of *Komsomol Easter*. What's more she gave me her icon of the Smolensk Virgin for keeps. On the back you could just make out the words in pencil: *Riza in memory of the miraculous cure* and the date — either *1841 or 1871*.

She taught me to give to the poor:

"It's harder to beg."

My relations with Granny were clouded only once. I liked the expression *You're eating our bread!* in Virta's *Laws* — and I worked it into the conversation. I suffered as a result. Mama shamed me while Granny pretended nothing had happened and went on treating me l i k e a b a b y :

"Eat up now, it's the last one. The last one is always the best."

I whined: "Any old dusty piece of candy would be better..."

Granny always had a piece of candy tucked away somewhere.

I was thinking of trading my silver ruble with the worker and the peasant on it for one apple — it didn't occur to me that an apple cost more then, far more.

Our half-witted Udelnaya lodger Varvara Mikhailovna brought me a carrot as a present: *for my bunny*. Moral torture: I couldn't accept the precious gift knowing that we still had some carrots left, so I hid under the table.

Physical torture: the gray mouse Megera — she had been allotted a room in Apt. 5 when it was turned into a communal apartment in the '20s — had lugged home a lot of castor-oil beans from the Moscow Region Land Department. She grudgingly gave us some. Then ate her fill and nothing happened to her. We were all sick to our stomachs. The next morning, Granny barely managed to drag herself into work. Mama was flat on her back the whole day. I felt nauseous till summer.

Grandfather was tall, his work was physical and a nervous strain as well. He made his way to and from work on foot. Hunger was hardest on him. Soon his red pocked face was redder still, his bright eyes even brighter from the headaches, and his shaven skull covered with old-mannish liver spots. He didn't so much walk as stagger. One day he fell down in the street. They brought him to Granny at Sklifosofsky. A month later I ran outside to watch Granny leading him slowly down Bolshaya Ekaterininskaya. Grandfather, who had fastened diamonds to marshals' stars, died of alimentary dystrophy after the Battle of Stalingrad, just before Easter. On his deathbed he kept saying:

"I'd like to see what's going to happen next. If only for a minute."

Mama/Granny conferred in whispers for a long time about how to be with me: the first dead person in my life.

Grandfather was cremated and the urn left in a common grave.

Granny explained to me that after the war there would be free trade and then there would be everything we needed.

There was nothing.

Professoror Yudin was imprisoned. At Sklifosovsky they explained:

"They arrested him at the aerodrome — he was trying to escape to America."

As always, Granny didn't believe a word of it.

How she aged! I remember her always in motion, ministering to all her family and friends. In my first photographs, she is little, bent and tired.

How she tried to keep up with me, to follow my passions! Gigli: Gigli. Vertinsky: Vertinsky. Balmont: Balmont. Futurism: Futurism. Perhaps it gave her strength...

In 1950 I discovered the poetry of Pasternak. I couldn't share this happiness with Mama or Papa. I thought Granny would be interested — on account of her memories — and I read her *The Lofty Malady*:

> In those days we all conceived a passion
> For storytelling, and winter through the nights
> Grew never tired of twitching from the lice,
> As horses twitch their ears...

> > Although the ceiling, as before,
> > In serving to support a cage,
> > Had dragged the second floor to the third,
> > And hoisted the fifth up to the sixth...
> > Yet plainly this was a forgery;
> > And through the water pipes' system
> > There mounted to the top that empty,
> > Breath-sucking scream of troubled times...
> > Which was more irksome than this verse,
> > And, rearing a mile into the air,
> > Did seem to grunt: "I say there, wait;
> > Was there something I did want to eat?"

> > > But there behind, in a blaze of legends,
> > > The hero, intellectual, and fool,

> In a fire of slogans and decrees,
> Burnt to the glory of the dark power
> Which, surreptitiously in corners,
> Ironically mocked and defamed him...

Granny listened intently and, when I had finished, became pensive: "His observations are all so true!"

Granny died — of a heart attack — on 17 October 1951. I went to 5a, Apt. 5, for the last time. A cooled jug of milk stood in a basin on the long oak table. My head was in the cinema-institute clouds: I didn't go to the funeral because of a frivolous rehearsal. No one said anything to me.

A man who had rented a room at Bolshaya Ekaterininskaya when he was a student wrote to Mama from the provinces:

> ...we are very glad therefore that you are well, glad the way one can only be glad for one's very dearest friends. And indeed, how can we forget you and the exceptionally beautiful mind and poetic soul of Irina Nikitichna and what must have been for her on the whole a difficult life. And how too bad and deeply unfair when we lose such good people as I.N., whose presence alone and even the fact that they are alive somewhere, that they exist, brightens your own life and inspires you to all sorts of good and kind deeds. About people such as that one can't help but recall Zhukovsky's words: "Say not that they are no longer, but with gratitude that they were!"

After Granny's death Mama held out for about six months. One night in early spring she got up, then fell backwards, onto her camp bed. The ambulance never came. In the morning a woman from the Sturtsel Policlinic turned up:

"What happened? She sick?"

"I jumped too far."

"Where'd you jump from?"

Mama, as far back as I can remember, sincerely believed that she was always exhausted because she pushed herself too hard:

"Yakov turned me into a hired hand. Just cried my eyes out at first..."

The work consisted of cooking/cleaning. Papa did most of the shopping. Now that Mama had taken to her bed, Papa came home from work every day and cooked regular meals with soup first and then a meat dish. As always there was no pleasing her.

Mama's long illness and convalescence,

my leaving the Cinema Institute for the Foreign Languages Institute (INYAZ),

the move from Kapelsky to distant Chapayev Lane,

my tumultuous life at INYAZ and the arrest of Chertkov,

my marriage and my leaving home,

Vera's suicide in the clinic,

my divorce and my second marriage,

and, finally, the distance and the years:

because of all this Bolshaya Ekaterininskaya gradually receded from Mama's memory — as did the common grave at the old crematorium where Grandfather and then Granny wound up. Mama lived simply and placidly.

Here is the letter she wrote Galya and me from Udelnaya when we were vacationing on the Baltic:

> Dear ones, I don't want to write. We'll see each other soon enough but I keep thinking you'll worry, not hearing from us in so long. Our life continues quiet, some days we feel better than others, like old people. I've made a lot of strawberry

jam and a little cherry. This year we have a lot of cherries, there will still be some on the trees when you return. We have a branch each of red and black currants, there are almost none at the market and very expensive — I didn't buy any. We have lots of apples, only small, like walnuts. You can eat them or, if you like, make jam. I've run out of sugar and don't have any jars. I felt a bit cross at Galya, she forgot to bring me the jars and lids, you still have them. I made a little raspberry jam. Just in time, it's been raining steadily, the rest of the raspberries have rotted on the bush. Except for Slesareva, no one has come out to see us from Moscow. It seems they've all grown old and don't have the strength to come to the country.

Andrei, when you're in Moscow, ask Lenochka what to take for sclerosis. Sometimes I totter to one side. I couldn't find the Diosponin before leaving. What else I haven't taken, I don't know. I must stop. Papa is in a hurry to leave for the market. I'm in a whirl the whole day, I get tired but have little to show for it. Ask your landlady if she hasn't any real wool socks anywhere. Because they're hard to find in Moscow. They have them at the peasant market, only I never go. Papa doesn't understand. Much love

The handwriting seems to be Mama's, or maybe it's Papa's. The letter is neither signed, nor dated. Outside time and space.

On Chapayev Lane, the other people in Mama's entrance were like her, only without Bolshaya Ekaterininskaya: right-thinking. Mama was afraid of them, just as she was afraid of everyone in life, but always joined in their endless discussions of not just the private lives of famous singers, Party officials, writers...

"I thought so! Chkalov's widow is going to marry Belyakov."

"Is it true Khrushchev, Sholokhov and Mao Zedong are married to sisters?"

"Listen to this joke I heard! Our Soviet tsars were: Vladimir the Wise, Joseph the Terrible and Nikita the Corn-lover."

After Papa's death, Mama moved in with us: she would rather starve or cadge something from the neighbors than bother to heat up the lunch left for her in the refrigerator. Our eleventh-floor windows on the former Fourth Meshchanskaya Street look out on the place where Bolshaya Ekaterininskaya used to be. Until the Olympics, in 1980, we could see three-story, brick 5a in the distance. It was demolished just before the opening. Mama couldn't be troubled to even glance in that direction.

About Bolshaya Ekaterininskaya: elucidation

Like any self-contained world, Bolshaya Ekaterininksaya had its own fixed ideas about how the outside world worked. Their essence could be reduced to four tenets:

1. *The truth is what I know myself or have heard from a friend, relation or neighbor.* A supposition, a rumor, a nice story or something read between the lines all turned into indisputable fact on the first retelling:

"that the Tsar's family and Nicholas II himself had survived. A beggar-woman from Pereyaslavka Street saw him at Leningrad Station. 'You know who I am, do you?' he said. 'Take this as a memento.' The beggar-woman produced a gold ten-ruble coin with his portrait."

Around 1945 Great Aunt Varya rented a room in suburban Kratovo with Margushka and her grandson. A colonel and his wife were living in the dacha next door: "I immediately thought it was the tsar's daughter." Her name was Tatiana Nikolaevna. Looked just like her father and, what's more, she had that same way of poking her finger"; ·

"that Lenin had pardoned the Socialist-Revolutionary Fanny Kaplan and that she now lived in a little house of her own on the Kolyma river;"

"that Lenin was a syphilitic — like Mayakovsky";

"that Stalin was a sadist and had shot his wife" — Bolshaya Ekaterininskaya had a soft spot for Alliluyeva and visited her grave;

"that Marshal Budyonny had shot his wife (a spy, supposedly), too, whereas Voroshilov had refused to let them arrest his — he defended her with a revolver";

"that Budyonny was a horse thief and Voroshilov a strikebreaker";

"that Oksana Petrusenko, the famous singer, became pregnant by Voroshilov and died having the abortion";

"that Lunacharsky, Molotov and Kalinin all loved ballerinas";

"that Kalinin secretly believed in God and held prayer services at home";

"that Rykov was a drunk: *Rykov went out for a pick-me-up, and came back falling down*";

"that all the political jokes were made up by Radek, but they couldn't shoot him because then who would write the front-page editorials in *Pravda* and *Izvestia*?";

"that the people in the Industrial Party and the 1937-38 show trials were all false victims: how could anyone say such awful things about himself?"

"that in Lubyanka there was this terrifying battle-ax — all higgledy-piggledy — a monster. If they let her into your cell, there was nothing you wouldn't sign";

"that Geltser, the ballerina, was an informer";

"that Meyerhold killed his wife, Zinaida Raikh, with an axe";

"that Vera Kholodnaya was cut up and thrown down a well";

"that Demyan Bedny was the son of a grand duke: Pridvorov;"

"that all the obscene verses were composed by the sweetest person in the world, Sergei Esenin."

2. *Lies are everything from official sources*: from the papers, from the radio, from those hateful Party meetings. This position was devoutly adhered to for twenty-five years until the regime's prestige, augmented by wartime victories, fused with the traditional suspicion of strangers. On Bolshaya Ekaterininskaya they went on and on about how:

"they'd caught an old woman hawking cutlets made of babies' flesh":

"a man was going around Moscow throwing little boys under trams: so our country would have fewer defenders."

From there it was just a step to killer-doctors:

"I was always afraid to put Andrei in the hospital, you just never know..."

3. *We're good, plain people; other people aren't like us.* Granny and Mama believed that other people were c u n n i n g, s e c r e t i v e and w i c k e d. Whereas they and t h e i r s were h o n e s t, f o r g i v i n g d u f f e r s:

"Only fools don't walk all over us."

At the same time, Mama had a good memory for bad turns and Granny had no scruples about getting what she wanted.

"O u r   k i n d , Russians, they *do things in a big way*:

If they're felling a tree, they raze the forest."

"They'll give you the shirt off their back, be it for food or for drink, no matter."

"Russians are reckless: Damaev ruined his voice with drink, sang to merchants in the freezing cold riding in a troika." And almost disapprovingly: "Chaliapin took good care of his voice."

"Russians are *talented*: Pushkin, Tolstoy. Naturally gifted. Vodka is everyone's downfall."

But not all Russians are o u r   k i n d. For instance:

"Country bumpkins."

"Former members of the nobility. They're like radishes: white on the inside, red on the outside. They all toady. Inform on anyone. The wretches."

"Sons of priests. From a priest's seed, don't expect a good breed. They're greedy and lying, just Russian Jews."

Jews were a separate matter. As far as Bolshaya Ekaterininskaya was concerned, the Revolution was the work of Jews. Granny referred to Litvinov as the Zionist sage. Stalin they always suspected of being Jewish, Lenin never: in his time the universal Yid was Trotsky. GPU heads — Dzerzhinsky, Menzhinsky, Yagoda, Ezhov — were above suspicion.

There were never any Jews on Bolshaya Ekaterininskaya.

They read disinterestedly of the Beiliss Affair and said, smugly: "That's the kind we are, didn't allow an innocent man to die."

They condemned pogroms, but also with detachment. They couldn't imagine themselves — and didn't try to — in the victims' place.

After the Revolution came the d o m i n a t i o n   o f   t h e   Y i d s:

"No matter where you look, they're everywhere. Two Yids in three gigs."

"They settle in and the next thing you know they're trying to bring in their kin."

To say *I am Russian* in the 1920s was almost the same as saying *I am a counterrevolutionary*. To say *you are a Jew* was almost the same as saying *I am an anti-Semite*.

Anyone on Bolshaya Ekaterininskaya would have objected to being called an anti-Semite. The heightened attention to suddenly prominent Jews came not of anti-Semitism, but of a vain effort to make sense of the situation:

"They're ready to live ten to a room and even so they don't feel crowded: it's a regular kahal."

"They haven't been here two minutes before they finagle a separate apartment."

"They never wash, they're dirty, they reek of rotten onions."

"They're so clean. Look at how they're always washing. Fresh shirts practically every day."

"They don't like to work. That's why they boss people, don't like to work."

"They're so hardworking. They don't make their wives work, they provide for everyone."

"They're smart. They teach their children to play the violin. You can't take a piano with you, but a violin you can tuck under your arm and run..."

"They're damned numbskulls. Can't get anything through their thick heads, have to be told ten times."

"They have a knack for languages: pick them up like that."

"They might learn at least not to murder Russian! Live their whole lives in Moscow and still talk like bumpkins."

"They hover over their children: '*Yashka, eat yur chicken fet!*' "

"Jews are worldly, practical people, they don't feel much when someone close to them dies."

Bolshaya Ekaterininskaya was coming to some conclusions: first of all, Jews themselves knew it was shameful to be Jewish:

"They go around grabbing up Russian surnames, then hide the fact."

Second of all, Jews were n o t a t a l l l i k e u s:

"On Sukkoth, whoever jumps the highest, his sins will be absolved."

"In the tram the other day I again heard them making a racket: *fir par portselin teller lakh.*"

"They don't like us..."

Bolshaya Ekaterininskaya was ready to like c u l t i v a t e d Jews, assimilated Jews, that is, Jews who weren't wild and wooly. Bolshaya Ekaterininskaya was even touched by Jews like that: they had arms and legs, human heads, knew Russian, they even had toothaches, just like normal people.

After the war, when Stalin drank to the Russian people, Bolshaya Ekaterininskaya understood what he meant, but didn't stop believing in the Y i d d i s h d o m i n a t i o n. When they heard that Jews were being fired or weren't being hired, they doubted it:

"They're just exaggerating."

"They're always complaining..."

They still wondered about every new person:

"He's not Jewish, is he?"

The Jews occupied far more space in their consciousness than all the other nationalities combined.

Besides Jews, living among the Russians there were Tatars, Chinese and Germans.

Bolshaya Ekaterininskaya remembered the Tatars *from that very time*, and gloated because now they were reduced to being yard-keepers and rag-and-bone men:

"Br-r-ring-da-ding! Bring us yer things!"

> Oh, oh, oh, and God forbid,
> You befriend Tatars, young misses,
> Soon those un-christened souls
> Will be stealing kisses.

After the *Revolushit*, Tatars suddenly became a danger:

"Whenever they come looking for someone, who do they go to? The yard-keeper. Whenever they search someone's room, who's sitting there as a witness? The yard-keeper..."

The Chinese danger was soon over and forgotten:

"I still remember how back in 1919 a c o o l i e was sitting on a curbstone, *scratching himself*. Caught a louse — and bit into it. Crunched it up and swallowed it: *'Shi-zya-shi iii......'*"

"That coolie was so good-natured, always walking around doing conjuring tricks. He'd press a little pipe against a bad tooth, say a charm — and pull out a worm: the tooth was cured."

"The Chinese ran laundries on Sretenka Street. Did a clean job and never cheated you..."

This verse survived in the yard up until the war:

> A German-pepper-mustard —
> Sauerkraut and sausage —
> Ate a herring without the tail
> Then said: 'I'll eat the pail!'

The Russian Germans — not Baltic Germans, not settlers of the Volga and the south, but city-dwellers of cultivated professions — were long gone.

Not surprisingly there was no one in China to notice the disappearance of the Chinese in Russia. What's astounding is that the German Germans didn't notice the disappearance of the Russian Germans.

Bolshaya Ekaterininskaya did not feel itself the equal of any nationality on earth.

The existence of Ukrainians and Byelorussians was subject to doubt.

Byelorussians: there aren't any.

Ukrainians: they're Russians, only Polonized, an example of Russians who a r e n o t o u r k i n d: very clean, cunning and tight-fisted. They call us butchers and Muskies. They murder the Russian language.

Moldavians: they're Gypsies, only they don't admit it. Gypsies always say:

"We're not Gypsies, we're Serbsies."

They treated Gypsies with a wary contempt:

"They're wild. They don't work: they're always begging and stealing. If they break in, they take everything..."

Yet their whole lives they would recall with an air of importance how: "A Gypsy woman once told me..."

The names of peoples in the Russian North and on the Volga sounded like curse words:

"Komis. Samoyeds. Tatars. Mordvinians."

Of the Balts, until '39 only the executioner Latvians were of concern. In 1939-40, they were all — Finns, Estonians, Latvians and Lithuanians — suddenly malicious: they hate us.

The romantic Georgians were seen in two hypostases. In Moscow they were sickly students, in Tbilisi they were *kintos* (street vendors):

"In the park one day, a young lady walked by wearing a cross round her neck. A kinto walked up and kissed the cross. She screamed. A policeman appeared. The kinto explained: 'When I sees de holy cross, I oways keess eet!' "

Armenians were all bootblacks. They lumped Armenians together with Assyrians.

Chechens, Circassians, Caucasian Tatars: they'd heard that if you so much as blinked, they'd go for their daggers.

Crimean Tatars: Bolshaya Ekaterininskaya had seen them in

the Crimea and respected them. They were good farmers, hardworking, honest.

Turkestan was "me-you-no-understand".

> One camel walks along,
> Another camel walks along,
> A third camel walks along,
> A whole caravan of camels walks along.

Yakuts were even worse.

Koreans were all spies.

The eastern borders were blurred in their minds. Living on the far side were simply:

Chinese: yellow, indigent, and lots of them. Their greatest revolutionary was Sun Ova-Gun.

Japs: puny and cruel. The bastards beat us.

> Togi, Mogi, Kamimuri
> Couldn't-wouldn't let us live.

Indians were wise and sedate. To be pitied, like Negroes.

Arabs were stately, noble.

Turks and Persians were Turks and Persians.

"Suvorov always beat the Turks."

"The Persians beat Griboyedov to death... And then they say they couldn't find him."

Our brother Slavs should like us. The Poles are traitors among Slavs because they don't. They're sleek on the outside, puffed up and intent on dazzling, but inside they're nothing and they lisp:

"Ne pepshi vepshu pepshem, ale peshepepshish vepshu pepshem."

Of all the great peoples of the West, the Germans were the closest and the most hated:

"Fat sausage-makers all of 'em, always gulping beer."

"Germans don't work the way we do. German exactitude. German technology."

"The Germans would sacrifice a man for the sake of order."

"Once there was a German stationed in our house — an officer — he gave us bread. Their bread is like rubber."

Englishmen were gaunt, stiff and straight as ramrods. English women were all old maids.

Frenchmen were frog-eaters who always clicked their heels. Frenchmen were like us, heartfelt and (sigh) cultivated. French women were afraid to give birth.

Italians were macaroni-eaters. With censure and affection:

"They all sing..."

Spaniards began to exist during their Civil War.

"How much we squandered on that glutton of a country."

America was wild and boorish, like Siberia. Odd coming from grandmothers/mothers raised on Fenimore Cooper, Edgar Allan Poe, Mark Twain and Jack London.

When she was still living with the Trubnikovs, Granny read *Uncle Tom's Cabin* and dreamed of marrying a Negro so she could have little black children. Into old age she loved to recall h o w T o p s y   d a n c e d .

Now and then, from out of Granny's exotic haze, there emerged:

"When a white woman comes to Madagascar, they adorn her with flowers."

"Life on Tahiti is paradise..."

It's interesting to compare when and whom the Russians

fought the last time in fact, and how it registered in Bolshaya Ekaterininskaya's mind.

ADVERSARY	IN FACT	IN MIND
Sweden	Early 19th century	Under Peter the Great
Finland	Second World War	Winter 1939-40
Poland	September 1939	Time of Troubles
England	Crimean War	Never
France	Crimean War	Under Napoleon
Italy	Second World War	Never
Austria	First World War	First World War
Germany	Second World War	Second World War
Hungary	Second World War	Never
Rumania	Second World War	Never
Bulgaria	First World War	Never
Turkey	First World War	Near Shipka and Plevna
Persia	1828-29	When Griboyedov was killed
China	Boxer Rebellion	Never
Japan	1945	1945
USA	Never	Never

The general tendency was to relegate any encounter with other peoples — even such a vivid and painful one as war — to the realm of legend. Other peoples did not demand the hourly attentions that our Jewish neighbors did. Suffice it to say that they were not like us.

So then:

1. *The truth is what I know myself or have heard from a friend, relation or neighbor.*

2. *Lies are everything from official sources.*

3. *We are good, plain people; others aren't like us.*

And finally, 4. *Evil is unavoidable and it's not up to us to fight it.*

At the sight of villainy, Bolshaya Ekaterininskaya hid, retreated into itself, was indignant — at pogrom leaders, at commissars, at informers, at the high and mighty — and endured it with a shrug:

"It can't be helped."

Without suspecting as much, Bolshaya Ekaterininskaya itself was just on the line between transgression and sanctity.

As a child I was disgusted by the quiet squalor of Bolshaya Ekaterininskaya. As a young man I despised it for being out-of-date. In the '60s, it began to draw me. Here and there the street had been touched up, tidied up. I began to see and understand what I hadn't been able to see and understand before.

> Perhaps I've finally grown kinder, sillier,
> I'm even ashamed to admit that living on hearsay,
> I once hurled threats at these wretched houses,
> Where boys, hanging off roofs with no purchase,
> Still race pigeons over Moscow,
>
> Where a pre-Soviet quiet reigns to this day,
> And old women stand in antediluvian garb
> While in each one's window in the sun,
> A cat lies frozen between the flowers,
> A languid cheek pressed against the pane.
>
> I enter into my father and grandfather's dream.
> On the corner, as always, is Sokolov's store,
> On Orlov, there's One-eyed Petka's stall,
> On Samara, there's Osterman-Tolstoy's Empire,
> A little lower down and behind it, the Union Stadium.
>
> I never knew you and yet I'll speak well of you:
> You are worthy parties in life's drama.
> Oh, if only I might somehow meet up with you!

...The old man with the artistic nostrils
Gingerly leading his lame-legged wife...

I am from here. And this fund of local ways
Will remain in me as a reality until the end.
I peer hopefully into faces unknown to me:
Perhaps in one a hint of recognition will flash,
In one consonant feelings will speak up?

Who here remembers me? Besides this winter,
Besides this street that has become my passion...
I used to dream like a puppy of getting even with it,
But now I'm afraid to take a deep breath,
Lest these frail houses come tumbling down.

Bolshaya Ekaterininskaya Street held out until 1976. The entire neighborhood, from Durov Street to Tryphonovskaya, was razed to make way for the Olympic complex. The odd person rummaged in the rubble. Enormous lindens and poplars lay sawed up, in rows, like timber.

1977-92

Andrei Sergeev and his wife Galina Muravyova at the 1997 Booker
reception. He has just been announced winner of the Booker Prize.

1891. When Grandfather turned eighteen, the matchmaker asked for his photograph. He and a friend clubbed together and had their picture taken on Tverskaya Street.

Right: Grandmother in 1890; during WWI; and in 1951.

The Sergeevs in 1910, the village of Zhukovka. Yakov is on the far right.

Gymnastics pyramid... Officers on the bottom.

Yakov Sergeev, a volunteer in the tsarist army. 1912.

Andrei Sergeev at 14 with his father Yakov.

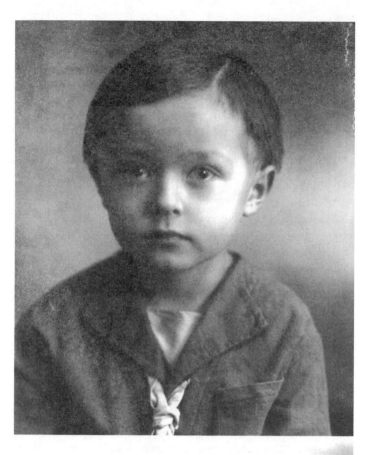

Andrei Sergeev's mother in the 1940s.

Top left: Andrei at 5.

Bottom left: Udelnaya.

Andrei Sergeev (top left) with Joseph Brodsky (bottom left) and the Golyshevs. 1970.

Andrei in 1973.

Andrei Sergeev in his study at home. 1996.
(photo by Pavel Gorshkov)

NOTES
by Natalya Vinyar

BEFORE THE WAR

p. 8   *Udelnaya* and *Malakhovka* are dacha settlements in the countryside about 40 km from Moscow.

p. 9   *Marxlen* — a name composed of 'Marx' and 'Lenin'

p.10   *Pushkin Anniversary* — the centennial of the death of the poet Alexander Pushkin (1799-1837).

p.10   *Marshal Voroshilov* — Kliment Voroshilov (1881-1969); a Civil War hero in Soviet mythology; from 1934 People's Commissar of Defense.

p.11   *THANK YOU COMRADE STALIN FOR OUR HAPPY CHILD-HOOD* — a slogan drummed into Soviet children from the mid '30s.

p.11   *Concise History of the Communist Party* (1938) was required reading for Soviet citizens, especially Chapter 4, part of which Stalin wrote.

p.11   *Turn the picture of Kalinin upside down and he looks like Radek* — Mikhail Kalinin (1875-1946), a longtime ally of Stalin's, officially head of the state; Karl Radek (1885-1939), former supporter of Trotsky, Party spokesman.

p.11   *They haven't shot [Radek] because then who would there be left to write the lead articles...* — At an open trial (1937), Radek was sentenced not to death, like others, but to ten years imprisonment; he soon died in camp, but rumor had it that he was alive and still writing articles.

p.11   Agnia Barto (1906-81), a popular children's writer.

p.12   *activist* — a local volunteer who does the authorities' bidding.

p.12   *the Red Study Corner* — A room set aside in apartment buildings and institutions for "cultural and educational" activities.

p.12   *They've arrested Hoffman for having a photograph of Trotsky* — Mass arrests on charges of Trotskyism continued till the end of the '30s.

p.12   *But they aren't a bit shy about calling our house the Big House* — "The Big House" was a euphemism (more in Leningrad, than in

Moscow) for the main building of the security organs (the Cheka, GPU, OGPU, NKVD, MVD, MGB, KGB).

p.12 *On the corner of First Meshchanskaya Street there used to be a church...* — In the 1930s, in Moscow alone several hundred churches were demolished as part of the anti-religious campaign under Marx's slogan: "Religion is the opium for the people."

p.12 *Papa is enchanted by new, modern First Meshchanskaya* — Almost no new apartment buildings were built in Moscow in the '30s. First Meshchanskaya (now Prospekt Mira) was renovated only because it led to the All-Union Exhibition of Agricultural Achievements, opened in 1939.

p.12 *a coatless man ... asks Mama for twenty kopecks* — Official propaganda did not recognize mass hunger or foster compassion; the word 'charity' was subject to censorship.

p.13 *a hot Mikoyan cutlet on a round roll* — Anastas Mikoyan (1895-1978), People's Commissar of Trade and the Food Industry (1926-46), introduced these Soviet hamburgers after a trip to the United States.

p.13 *Brockhaus and Efron* — the most authoritative pre-revolutionary Russian encyclopedia, 86 volumes (St. Petersburg: 1890-1907).

p.13 *Small Soviet Encyclopedia* — An encyclopedia in 10 volumes (1930-32).

p.13 *Papa doesn't cut articles out of the Encyclopedia or paste over pictures* — Articles about persons declared "enemies of the people" were supposed to be removed from books by the books' owners themselves.

p.14 *Timiryazev* — Klimenty Timiryazev (1843-1920), natural scientist, long a professor at the Peter the Great Agricultural Academy, later renamed the Timiryazev Agricultural Academy.

p. 14 *Dyman has taken to turning up in church... and spying out acquaintances* — College-level teachers could be fired for going to church.

p.14 *"Sadist! Syphilitic!"* — 'Sadist' refers to Stalin, 'syphilitic' to Lenin. Officially Lenin died of sclerosis, but unofficially it was believed that he died of syphilis complications.

p.14 *I said my papa was a tsarist general* — An unmasked tsarist general could be deprived of his civil rights, sent into exile or arrested.

p.15 *cubes, rectangles, four diamonds with a star, red cuffs, chevrons on sleeves* — These signs of distinction were introduced after the Revolution; the former signs — shoulder straps — were initially done away with as symbols of the tsarist army, but reinstated in 1943.

p.15 Marshal Semyon Budyonny (1883-1973), a legendary Civil War hero in Soviet mythology; his long handlebar moustache was his most remarkable feature.

p.15 *The spire on the Budyonny helmet is a military ruse* — In fact, Budyonny's First Cavalry Army had inherited Old Russian-style pointed helmets made for the tsarist army.

p.15 *Raskova... Grizodubova... Osipenko* — The first Soviet women pilots; celebrated for their non-stop flight from Moscow to the Russian Far East (1938).

p.15 *Otto Yulevich Shmidt, Captain Voronin* — Leaders of the expedition of the *Chelyuskin*, a ship bound from Murmansk to Vladivostok non-stop, but trapped by ice (1934) in the Sea of Okhotsk.

p.15 *Molokov, Kamanin, Lyapidevsky, Levanevsky* — pilots who participated in the rescue of the *Chelyuskin*.

p.15 *Chkalov, Baidukov, Belyakov* — pilots who made the first non-stop flight from Moscow to the United States over the North Pole (1937).

p.15 *Gromov, Yumashev, Danilin* — pilots who flew non-stop from Moscow to the United States over the North Pole (1937).

p.16 *Papanin, Krenkel, Shirshov, Fyodorov* — Polar explorers who worked aboard the first Soviet drift-ice station (1937-38).

p.16 *The most important is Valery Chkalov* — Chkalov (1904-38), the famous hero-pilot, developed new figures in acrobatic flying. The circumstances of Chkalov's death during a test flight remain unclear; some said Stalin had a hand in it.

p.16 *The Tatar yard-keeper's family may be eyeing it...* — Tatar yard-keepers lived in the basements and semi-basements of many Moscow apartment buildings in the '30s, '40s and '50s.

p.16 *Tatar rag-and-bone men* — Since before the Revolution rag-and-bone men were often Tatars.

p.16 *Nannies are everywhere* — The hungry countryside supplied nannies in abundance.

p.17 *rooster lollipops — a mother's nightmare* — Lollipops were homemade; some mothers also suspected that their peddlers licked them to make them shine.

p.18 *Sokolov's* — A store referred to by the name of its pre-revolutionary owner.

p18. *Mosselprom* — a state trust: "Moscow Association of Enterprises for Processing Agricultural and Industrial Produce".

p.19 *On the radio they're giving a lecture: Did the garden of Gethsemane really exist?* — The question was rhetorical and the radio program deeply atheist.

p.19 *Every morning I listen to a children's program... I'm always spellbound* — Children's radio programs and literature flourished in the '30s when they became a refuge for many talented writers and poets.

p.19 *Khetagurova girls* — Valentina Khetagurova (b. 1914) went to the Russian Far East and married a military man stationed there; thousands of girls followed her example in response to her appeal (1937) to "open up" this remote territory, but in fact to make up for the shortage of women there.

p.20 *Pavlik Morozov* — A boy who denounced his father to the authorities for resisting collectivization, Morozov (1918-32) was glorified in literature, opera and film. His action was typical of a time when many children renounced parents convicted as enemies of the people. According to a 1934 law, non-denunciation by family members over the age of 12 was punishable by 5-10 years' imprisonment if they knew about the "crime" and if they did not, by deprivation of rights and exile.

p.20 *Papa takes me for a ride on the metro* — The metro was conceived as a great socialist achievement, its stations (the first one opened in 1935) decorated with marble, bronze statues, and mosaics.

p.20 *the Kremlin... with its ruby stars* — A principal Soviet symbol, ruby stars replaced the double-headed eagles on the Kremlin towers in 1937.

p.20   *Over the November holidays Papa takes me to see the illuminations*
— The illuminations included slogans and a spectacular light panel that created the impression of movement (e.g. a combine against a background of waving grain.)

p.20   *I'm voting ... for Bulganin* — As usual, there was only one candidate on the ballot. Nikolai Bulganin (1895-1975), was elected to the Supreme Soviet in December 1937, and was a top member of the Soviet leadership until 1958.

p.21   *Scrawny, hungry Nyusha the milkmaid* — Peasants received next to nothing from collective farms. They were allowed to keep a bit of livestock of their own, but the income from it was cancelled out by exorbitant taxes and state requisitions.

p.22   *by a private physician, recommended by friends* — Private medical practices were only semi-legal in the '30s and gradually disappeared altogether.

p.24   Dmitry Bortnyansky (1721-1825), Russian composer mainly known for his religious music.

p.25   *Shulgin's Days* — A memoir by Vasily Shulgin (1878-1976), a politician and monarchist, who emigrated in 1920. *Days*, about the monarchy's overthrow, was published abroad in 1922 and in Moscow in 1926 after Shulgin (possibly associated with the OGPU) visited the USSR in secret.

p.25   *Higher and Higher, Bike Tour March, Divers' March, A Komsomol Member is Piloting the Plane* — Songs from the patriotic Soviet repertoire of the '30s.

p.25   Sergei Lemeshev (1902-77), lyrical tenor, soloist at the Bolshoi.

p.25   Ivan Kozlovsky (1900-93), lyrical tenor, soloist at the Bolshoi.

p.25   Vadim Kozin (1903-94), a popular singer of Russian and Gypsy songs in the '20s, '30s and '40s; after labor camp (1944-50), settled in Magadan.

p.25   Leonid Utyosov (1895-1982), popular variety singer and jazz orchestra conductor; infused jazz with Jewish-Odessan themes; switched to a Soviet lyrical and patriotic repertoire in the '40s.

p.25 *Varlamov* — Jazz composer and conductor (1904-1990); sentenced to labor camp and exile (1943-56).

p.26 *Pyatnitsky Choir* — A Russian folk choir created in 1910 by Mitrofan Pyatnitsky (1864-1927), a pillar of official art under Stalin.

p.27 Vyacheslav Molotov (1890-1986), chairman of the USSR Council of People's Commissariats (1930-41); People's Commissar of Foreign Affairs (1939-49 and 1953-56). Removed from office by Khrushchev in 1962.

p.27 *"No more using the word 'fascist' as a term of abuse"* — In August 1939 Germany and the USSR signed a non-aggression pact, soon supplemented by an agreement on friendship and borders.

p.28 *in Western Byelorussia and Lithuania they were not glad to see the Red Army* — The Red Army occupied Western Byelorussia (September 1939), Lithuania (June 1940), Latvia and Estonia (1940) in accordance with the Nazi-Soviet non-aggression pact's secret protocols, which gave the USSR free reign in Eastern Poland, the Baltic States, Finland and Bessarabia. In the USSR, the occupation was portrayed as aid to people who had greeted the Soviet forces with open arms.

p.28 *Red October* — a Moscow candy factory, one of the best in the USSR.

p.28 *the war with Finland* — In 1939, the rejection of the USSR's territorial claims in Finland led to the Winter War, which Finland lost.

p.28 *after the armistice* — The armistice between Finland and the USSR was signed on 12 March 1940.

p.28 *Vyborg* — a Finnish city ceded to the USSR as a result of the armistice.

p.28 *Schutzkorps* — A Finnish rifle corps (1917-44).

p.28 *Ogonyok* — an illustrated weekly magazine.

p.30 *The last tsar was Nicholas the Third* — an amalgam of the last tsar (Nicholas the Second) and his father (Alexander the Third).

p.31 *Artek* — an international Young Pioneer camp in the Crimea; a symbol of "happy" childhood in the USSR.

p.31 *they talk about the Arctic on the radio all the time* — Sea and air expeditions to the Arctic (1930-37) were celebrated as heroic feats of the Soviet people.

p.36 *Mannerheim line* — A system of fortifications (1927-39) along Finland's border with the USSR; named after the Finnish field marshal and statesman Baron von Mannerheim (1867-1951).

THE WAR

p.39 *WHITE GUARD FINLAND* — The Finnish White Army suppressed a revolutionary uprising in Finland in 1918.

p.39 *FASCIST LATVIA, ESTONIA, LITHUANIA* — authoritarian regimes were established in Lithuania (1926), Latvia (1934) and Estonia (1934).

p.39 Yefim Zozulya (1891-1941), author of several collections of stories, mainly satirical.

p.40 *black Caproni* — an Italian-made plane with which Italy supplied Franco during the Spanish Civil War (1936-39).

p.40 Boris Yefimov (1900-2001), a political cartoonist and creator of many political posters.

p.40 *Khetagurova girls* — See note to page 19.

p.40 *three tank drivers* — the eponymous heroes of a popular song.

p.40 *Karatsupa the border guard and his dog Hindu* — Border guard Nikolai Karatsupa (1910-94) was promoted as a hero during the years of the slogan: "Our Borders Must Be Under Lock and Key".

p.40 Arkady Gaidar (1904-41), author of Soviet classics for teenagers, including *A Military Secret* and *Timur and His Team*.

p.41 Sergei Mikhalkov (b. 1913), author of popular children's verses and of the lyrics to the Soviet anthems of 1944 and 1977 as well as the Russian anthem of 2000.

p.41 *FASCIST JAPAN has attacked good CHINA* — Japan occupied a significant part of China in 1937.

p.41 *the bogatyr Ezhov* — Nikolai Ezhov (1895-1940); People's Commissar of the NKVD (1936-38); organizer of mass purges (1937-38); nicknamed "the bloody dwarf." Poets in Soviet Central Asia glorified him as a *bogatyr* (mighty warrior).

p.41   Zhu De (1886-1976), Chinese leader, Army commander from 1931; organized the 6,000-mile Long March to Shanxi (1934-35).

p.41   *to attack us at Lake Hasan* — The USSR's Special Far Eastern Army suffered enormous losses when Japan attacked at Lake Hasan (1938); commanding officer Marshal Blyukher was shot that same year.

p.41   *On the Halhin-Gol River, the Japanese attack the Mongolian People's Republic* — In 1939 Japanese units invaded Mongolia near the Halhin-Gol river. Soviet forces drove them out.

p.41   *This is our one friendly border* — Formally, Mongolia was the USSR's ally; in fact, it was beholden.

p.42   *Voroshilov* — See note to page 10.

p.42   *Everyone's signed up to contribute to OSOAVIAKHIM* — Contributions to Osoaviakhim, a defense fund created in 1927, were supposedly voluntary but actually compulsory.

p.42   *Voroshilov marksmen* — sharpshooters who had earned this title and a Voroshilov badge.

p.43   *Beck and Rydz-Smigly* — Jozef Beck (1894-1944), Polish foreign minister (1932-39); and Edward Rydz-Smigly (1886-1941), commander of the Polish Army in 1939.

p.43   *Gold, gold is falling from the sky* — A line from the well-known poem *Summer Rain* by Apollon Maikov (1821-97).

p.44   *Instead of Czechoslovakia, there is simply Slovakia* — In 1939, Hitler occupied the Czech Republic while Slovakia was proclaimed an "independent state under German protection".

p.44   *The papers repeatedly confirmed our friendship. At noon on June 22 Molotov announced how it ended* — Germany attacked the USSR on 22 June 1941 at 4:15 a.m. Molotov made a radio announcement at noon. Stalin said nothing until 3 July.

p.44   *Kishinev* — The capital of Moldavia.

p.44   *no reports about Minsk and Smolensk* — Minsk fell on 28 June 1941, Smolensk (200 miles from Moscow) on 16 July.

p.44   *That summer — not the usual time — they awarded the Stalin Prize* — The Stalin Prize was instituted on 20 December 1939 in honor of Stalin's sixtieth birthday; it was awarded around that date thereafter.

p.44 Andrei Kostikov (1899-1950) received the Stalin Prize for the invention of the Katiusha (a truck-mounted multi-rail rocket launcher) which in fact was invented and developed by a group of his subordinates who were soon sent to gulags; the survivors were awarded 25 years later.

p.45 "I don't know where to evacuate to — the Ukraine, Tashkent, or Kislovodsk" — The Ukraine was occupied by the fall of 1941, Kislovodsk (Northern Caucasus) by August 1942.

p.45 "Levanevsky didn't die at the North Pole"— Sigismund Levanevsky (1902-37), a pilot, perished trying to fly over the North Pole.

p.45 Count Alexei Tolstoy (1882-1945), author of original prose in the '10s and '20s, Soviet novels in the '30s, and newspaper articles during the war.

p.46 Julio Jurenito — The Extraordinary Adventures of Julio Jurenito (1922), a satirical novel by Ilya Erenburg (1891-1967).

p.46 And if they come and evict us — During the war it seemed quite possible that dachas might be requisitioned; in reality, only cars, motorcycles, and radio sets were.

p.47 Shafran is an obviously Jewish name, Akimov is obviously Russian.

p.48 a volunteer corps — of these corps' hundreds of thousands of volunteers — untrained and poorly armed — few survived.

p.52 The Stamp from the Land of Gondeloupa — A children's story, popular in the '30s and '40s, by Sophia Mogilevskaya.

p.52 Hedgehog (Yozh) — A children's monthly magazine, published in Leningrad (1928-35).

p.53 Just an Ordinary Horse by Shershenevich — A collection of verses (1920) by the theoretician and co-founder of Russian Imagism Vadim Shershenevich (1893-1942).

p.53 The Germans were supposed to arrive ...on the 16th of October — On 15 October 1941, following the news about the Russian army's defeat at Vyazma, panic set in in Moscow and Muscovites began evacuating in droves. The Germans came very close to Moscow. In December they were thrown back from Moscow.

p.53 a train carrying the government had left the metro — The Soviet government evacuated to the city Kuibyshev (now Samara). A secret metro line did exist.

p.53 *"Yelnya, Yelnya, all this fuss about Yelnya!* — Battles were then raging in Yelnya, a town in the Smolensk Region.

p.54 *Life isn't worth living / Without its delights...* — from the Duke's aria in Verdi's opera *Rigoletto* (1851).

p.57 *A Cloud in Pants* — a narrative poem (1915) by Vladimir Mayakovsky (1893-1930).

p.57 *the brisk, bright word Futurism* — Russian Futurism, a literary movement, developed in the 1910s by Velimir Khlebnikov, David Burlyuk and Vladimir Mayakovsky.

p.57 *I couldn't believe that Erenburg was the same Erenburg...* — The author of *Julio Jurenito* had turned to writing Soviet novels in the '30s and anti-Nazi articles during the war.

p.58 *Horthy, Ryti, Antonescu, Nedic, Quisling and Laval* — Admiral Nicholas Horthy (1868-1957), regent of Hungary (1920-44); Risto Ryti, Finnish prime minister (1939-40) then president (1940-44), convicted of war crimes (1946-49); Ion Antonescu (1882-1946), Rumanian dictator (1940-44), executed for war crimes (1946); Milan Nedic (1877-1946), head of the Serbian government (1941-44), arrested in 1946, committed suicide; Vidkun Quisling (1887-1945), head from 1933 of the Norwegian Fascist Party, made premier by Hitler (1942), executed as traitor (1945); Pierre Laval (1883-1945), French prime minister (1931-32 and 1935-36), head of Vichy government (1942-44), executed for treason (1945).

p.58 Demyan Bedny (real name Efim Pridvorov, 1883-1945), Soviet poet, satirist and propagandist.

p.67 *camp at Belomor* — Belomor, or the White-Baltic canal (opened in 1933) was the GULag's first great construction project.

p.68 *It didn't occur to the Leningraders to tell us about the seige* — Soviet propaganda celebrated Leningraders' heroism during the seige (July 1941-January 1944) but understated the real number of victims (around 1 million) as well as the horrors of hunger and cold.

p.68 Grigory Kotovsky (1881-1925), a criminal turned Civil War hero; his image was memorable due to the film *Kotovsky* (1943).

THE COMMUNAL APARTMENT

p.72 *THE COMMUNAL APARTMENT* — In the '20s, apartments were forcibly "consolidated" or made communal: the former owners (if they remained) retained one or two rooms; the other rooms went to other families; kitchen and bath/WC were shared.

p.73 *the Nirnzee house* — a 10-story "skyscraper" (1913) in the center of Moscow, designed by Ernest Nirnzee (ca. 1860-1918).

p.73 *Khitrov Market* — a famous Moscow market surrounded by flophouses (sheltering some 10,000 homeless) all razed in 1923.

p.74 *just like an Englishwoman out of Chekhov* — See Chekhov's short story "A Daughter of Albion" (1883).

p.74 *nepman* — a private entrepreneur during the New Economic Policy (see note to page 165).

p.75 *the Nemirovich* — A music studio founded (1919) by the famous director Vladimir Nemirovich-Danchenko (1858-1943); since 1926 the Nemirovich-Danchenko Music Theater.

p.75 *cinema newspapers from the '20s* — The illustrated bi-weekly *Sovetsky Ekran* (Soviet Cinema).

p.79 Alexander Vertinsky (1889-1957), a popular chansonnier in a decadent manner; lived in emigration in1920-43 but was allowed to resume his career upon returning to the USSR.

p.80 Candidate of Sciences — In Russia, the first academic degree awarded on defending a dissertation and allowing one to hold positions up to Associate Professor; the next and highest degree is that of a Doctor with which one can claim a full professorship.

p.82 *Stay In Your Own Lane... Guilty Without Guilt* — Two plays (1853; 1884) by Alexander Ostrovsky (1823-1886).

p.82 *the new Soviet anthem* — Commissioned by Stalin in1943 (lyrics by Sergei Mikhailkov and El-Registan, music by Alexander Alexandrov). After the Revolution, the Socialist "Internationale" was used by the Bolsheviks as their anthem.

p.82 *Lemeshev and Kozlovsky* — See note to page 25.

p.82 *broadcasts featured works that were cultural and comprehensible* — Tchaikovsky (*The Queen of Spades, Eugene Onegin, Iolanta*);

Wagner (*Lohengrin*); Rubinstein (*The Demon*); J. Strauss (*Der Zigeunerbaron*); Donizetti (*L'elisir d'amore*); Glinka (*Ruslan and Ludmila*); Gounod (*Faust*); Mozart (*The Barber of Seville, The Marriage of Figaro*); Mussorgsky (*Boris Godunov, The Hovansky Affair*); Rimsky-Korsakov (*Sadko*); Bizet (*The Pearl Fishers*); Offenbach (*La Perichole*); Kalman (*Silva*); Dargomyzhsky (*Rusalka*); Bizet (*Carmen*); Musical comedy (*Arshin Mal-Alan*).

p.85　Special stores, closed to all but the Soviet nomenklatura, began to multiply in 1931 when the so-called "campaign against wage-leveling" legalized significant social inequality. Goods there were sold at special low prices or distributed free.

p.87　*Metropolitan Philipp's rotunda* — a church in the classical style designed by Matvei Kazakov (1738-1812); restored and reopened in the '90s (a memorial service was held there on December 1, 1998, for the author of this book).

p.88　Vasily Zhukovsky (1783-1852); the poet and older friend of Pushkin's.

p.88　*the kitchen asked Klara Ivanovna to put in a good word for it when the Germans came* — Klara Ivanovna was Latvian and historically the Latvians had lived under Baltic German landowners.

p.88　*Kursk natives descended from Ukrainians sent there under Catherine the Great* — Catherine the Great gave vast tracts of land to Ukrainian Cossack leaders in a bid to stifle their independence.

p.89　*those cadets were the ones who defended the Kremlin in 1917* — After the Bolsheviks overthrew the Provisional Government in Petrograd on October 25 (November 7, New Style), armed conflicts began in Moscow. Cadets held the Kremlin until November 3 (November 16, NS).

p.90　*"When the White cavalry rode into Kursk ..."* — The cavalry of White General Denikin entered Kursk in the fall of 1919.

p.90　*Nemirovich* — See note to page 75.

p.90　*Zoya Kosmodemyanskaya* — a young partisan (1923-41) caught by the Germans near Moscow, tortured and hung.

p.90　*Christmas Eve* — a ballet based on Gogol's *Evenings on a Farm Near Dikanka*; music by Rimsky-Korsakov (1844-1908).

p.91 *"Sholokhov didn't write Quiet Don himself..."*— Mikhail Sholokhov (1905-1984), Nobel Prize winner (1965), was suspected of having plagiarized *Quiet Flows the Don* when the first volume came out (1928); the question remains.

p.93 VEF — radio factory in Riga which made the best radio sets in the USSR.

p.93 *FED*— a photo camera named for Felix Edmundovich Dzerzhinsky (1877-1926), founder of the Cheka (1917).

p.93 *Field of Kulikovo* — Site of the battle (1380) that marked the beginning of Russia's liberation from the Tatar-Mongol Yoke.

p.93 *Suvorov-like custodian*— Count Alexander Suvorov (1730-1800), the Russian generalissimo, was lean, agile and not very tall.

p.93 *Fet ... SHENSHIN ... the old men he had met there remembered the landowner but knew nothing of the poet*— The poet Afanasy Fet (1820-1892) was the son of a Russian nobleman, Afanasy Shenshin. But because his parents' marriage was not made legal until 1822, he could not use his father's name. Fet was the name of his mother.

p.93 *Tychina ... Zagul ... Rylsky ... Semenko*— Pavlo Tychina (1891-1967); Dmitro Zagul (1890-1938); Maksim Rylsky (1895-1964); Mikhail Semenko (1892-1937): pre-revolutionary poets of the Ukrainian avant-garde. In the '20s and '30s, Tychina and Rylsky gradually conformed to the Soviet mold; Zagul died in camp; Semenko was shot.

p.93 Velimir Khlebnikov (1885-1922), a poet and founder of Russian Futurism; experimented with words; introduced the concept of beyond-sense language (*zaum'*).

p.93 *Bryusov's institute* — A short-lived literary institute (1922-25) created by the Symbolist poet Valery Bryusov (1873-1924).

p.94 *the notorious 1948 session of the Academy of Agricultural Sciences*— In 1948, at Stalin's behest, Trofim Lysenko (1898-1976), president of the Academy of Agricultural Sciences (1938-56 and 1961-62), condemned genetics as a reactionary science; many selectionists, geneticists and biologists were arrested.

p.94 *...Lysenko — it's Lamarckism!"*— in his erroneous theory of the inheritance of acquired characteristics Lysenko had adopted certain ideas of Jean Baptiste Lamarck (1744-1829).

p.94 *Stalin's Marxism and Linguistics... Marr* — Stalin's 1950 brochure *Marxism and Linguistics* savaged the work of Nikolai Marr (1865-1934), until then an officially recognized authority.

FATHER

p.96 *turned into a communal apartment* — See note to page 71.

p.98 *the Foreign Trade Store* — A store where goods were sold only for gold or foreign currency.

p.101 Nikolai Nekrasov (1821-1878), a poet noted for civic stance, particularly his verses depicting the hard life of the Russian peasant.

p.101 *Balmont and Severyanin* — Konstantin Balmont (1867-1942), a Symbolist poet; Igor Severyanin (1887-1941), a poet and originator of Ego-Futurism; both emigrated after 1917.

p.102 *Aleksandrov Military Choir* — a Soviet Army ensemble created (1928) by Alexander Aleksandrov (1883-1946), who wrote the music to the Soviet Anthem.

p.102 Leonid Sobinov (1872-1934), lyric tenor at the Bolshoi (1897-1933).

p.102 *Shuisky in Boris Godunov* — Prince Shuisky, a character in the opera (1869) by Modest Mussorgsky (1839-81) based on the tragedy by Pushkin.

p.103 *Count Paskevich* — Count Ivan Paskevich (1782-1856), viceroy and commander in chief in the Caucasus (1827-30) during Russia's wars with Persia and Turkey.

p.107 *My father would have been happy never to have heard of [Akhmatova] his whole life* — Even non-readers of poetry would have heard of Anna Akhmatova (1889-1966) after the 1946 Central Committee resolution branding her work as alien to the people and to socialism.

p.108 *droshky* — an open carriage for one or two.

p.108 Vlas Doroshevich (1864-1922), satirical writer, author of many books including *Sakhalin: The Penal Colony* (1903).

p.109   *The Marriage* — a stage comedy (subtitled "A Completely Improbable Event in Two Acts") by Nikolai Gogol (1809-52).

p.109   *a descendant of Gogol-Yanovksy's* — The Gogol-Yanovskys were related to the writer Gogol.

p.109   Dmitry Mendeleev (1834-1907), the chemist who discovered the periodic system of the elements.

p.110   *Our own good soldier Svejk* — the eponymous hero of the Czech writer Jaroslav Hasek.

p.110   *Maria Fyodorovna* — Empress Maria Fyodorovna (1759-1828), the second wife of Paul I, created a number of charities and educational organizations. Empress Maria Fyodorovna (1847-1928), wife of Alexander III, continued these projects.

p.111   *"Cadets from the Kremlin"* — See note to page 89.

p.112   *Constituent Assembly* — Elections to the Constituent Assembly were scheduled for before the October Revolution, but took place afterwards. The Bolsheviks failed to win a majority and disbanded the Assembly the morning after its opening session (5 January 1918).

p.113   The Provisional Government was formed after the February Revolution and overthrown by the Bolsheviks in October 1917.

p.113   *23 February 1918* — a national holiday (Red Army Day). Demobilization on that day might have been misunderstood.

p.115   *a minister on the Samara Committee of Constituent Assembly Members* — This short-lived committee, formed in June 1918 in the Volga city of Samara by Socialist-Revolutionary members of the disbanded Assembly, rejected Bolshevik power and saw itself as a lawful government.

p.115   *Margarita Fofanova — the one who hid Lenin, and for whom Lenin left a note the night of October 24 (1917)* — Lenin had been wanted by the Provisional Government on charges of treason since July 1917; Fofanova (1883-1976) hid him in her apartment until October 24, the night before the Revolution, when he slipped out to Bolshevik headquarters at the Smolny Institute.

p.120   Sergei Vavilov (1891-1951), physicist, author of fundamental research in optics, president of the USSR Academy of Sciences (1945-51); brother of Nikolai Vavilov (see note to page 137).

p.120   Ivan Popov (1888-1964), livestock specialist, Academician.

p.121   *chervonets* — a banknote worth 10 rubles; the gold chervonets was part of a successful monetary reform (1922-24) that made the ruble convertible.

p.123   *Volunteer* — person with a secondary education serving a term in the tsarist army under priviledged conditions.

p.123   *oh, horrors! — a cooperative* — Successful before the Revolution, the independent cooperative movement was declared hostile to socialism by the Soviet regime; leaders of cooperative movement were arrested on charges of sabotage.

p.123   Prince Pyotr Kropotkin (1842-1921), anarchist philosopher, geographer; emigrated in 1876, returned after the February Revolution (1917), condemned the Bolshevik Revolution as "new Jacobinism".

p.123   *Pavel was rounded up during collectivization's first swipe* — Forced collectivization began in 1929, tapered off in 1930 (after Stalin's hypocritical article in favor of its being voluntary), then picked up again with greater force.

p.125   Fyodor Gladkov (1883-1958), Soviet writer, best known for his novel *Cement.*

p.125   Andrei Bely (1880-1934), leading theorist and poet of Russian Symbolism, also known for his novel *St Peterburg.*

p.125   *Belomor Canal* — See note to page 67

p.125   *Ukraine's most terrible famine* occurred in 1933 due to forced collectivisation and mass deportation of wealthy peasants (dekulakisation), as well as a severe draught and inept management; some people believed that the famine had been allowed to happen for purposes of intimidation.

p.126   *in '37 and '38... he woke up every time a car stopped outside* — The mass arrests of 1937-38 affected every level of society.

p.128   *on 29 August 1939 — just after the Soviet-German Pact* — See note to page 27.

p.128   *Candidate's degree* — See note to page 80

p.130   *Soviet Champagne* — sparkling wine produced according to Soviet technology and billed as an important achievement of socialism.

p.130   *Stalin laureate* — a winner of the Stalin Prize (see note to page 44).

p.130   *special store* — see note to page 85.

p.131   *a Stalin cow (a goat)* — A Stalin cow was a goat because under Stalin actual cows had first been taken away to collective farms (during collectivization) and later taxed so heavily that their owners were often compelled to sell or slaughter them.

p.131   *Sarapul* — a city on the Kama River, a tributary of the Volga.

p.132   *Long Ago* — a musical based on the play (1941) by Alexander Gladkov (1912-72); music by Tikhon Khrennikov (b. 1913).

p.132   *second-hand store* — Known as *komissionye*, these stores were especially attractive given the shortage of almost everything; private individuals brought new and old clothes there to sell, as well as home appliances, china, paintings, furniture, musical instruments, etc.

p.134   *Russia had the greatest freedom* — the period between the February and the October revolutions of 1917.

p.135   *I was trying to see in the Baltics an alternative to Soviets* — This attitude towards the Baltic republics made them a sort of Mecca for young people who went there for a taste of the West, of another life, unspoiled by socialism.

p.135   Tiit Kuuzik, opera singer (1911-1990), with the Estonia Theater in Tallinn from 1940, played Onegin in Chaikovsky's *Eugene Onegin*.

p.135   Pavel Khokhlov (1854-1919), opera singer, played the role of Onegin.

p.135   *Lubyanka* — Named for the square on which it stands, the Lubyanka was the name of the internal prison and the unofficial name of the residence of the Soviet security organs (from the Cheka to the KGB).

p.136   *living the four of us in one room, but we couldn't find anything to rent* — In Moscow and other big cities most young couples had no alternative but to live in one room with their parents, even after having their own children. Construction of apartment buildings began only under Khrushchev in the late '50s.

p.137   *Chayanov and Kondratev* — Professors at the Timiryazev Agricultural Academy, they were convicted in 1930 of involvement in "a counterrevolutionary Labor Party"; both died in camp. Alexander Chayanov (1888-1937), economist, an advocate of the cooperative movement, author of post-Symbolist prose and a utopian novel. Nikolai Kondratev (1892-1938), economist, author of the theory of "big cycles" in economic development.

p.137   Dmitry Pryanishnikov (1865-1948), agrochemist, studied under Timiryazev, founded a scientific school, from 1895 taught at the Agricultural Academy.

p.137   Nikolai Ivanovich Vavilov (1887-1943), brother of Sergei Vavilov (see note to page 118), biologist, geneticist, first president of the Academy of Agricultural Sciences (1929-35). Defended genetics against his successor Lysenko (see note to page 94); was arrested, died in prison.

p.137   Alexander Chizhevsky (1897-1964), biophysicist, archaeologist, imprisoned (1942-58).

p.137   *who's to blame for the collapse of agriculture in the Ukraine!* — Khrushchev ran the Ukraine from 1937-48.

p.137   Dmitry Polyansky (b. 1917), member of the Politburo (1960-76), responsible for agriculture under Khrushchev and later.

p.137   *Samuil Georgievich, a Jew, flew at him* — Such outspokenness was riskier for a Jew than a Russian.

p.139   *the House of Unions, of its columns in all their glory* — an 18th-century building in the classical style by Matvei Kazakov; formerly home to the Club of the Nobility.

BOLSHAYA EKATERININSKAYA

p.143   *Tverskaya Street* — Moscow's centralmost thoroughfare leading to the Kremlin.

p.146   Victor Vasnetsov (1848-1926), painter known for his fairytale themes.

p.148   *the Moscow uprising of 1905 ...Presnia district* — The Moscow uprising (December 1905) involved not only armed rebel militias, but thousands of workers who built barricades. The fiercest battles were fought in the Presnia district.

p.148 *Russkoye Slovo (a Sytin paper...)* — A liberal daily paper (1895-1918), published by Ivan Sytin (1851-1934), one of the largest publishers at the time.

p.148 *it had variety, from Doroshevich to Rozanov and Blok* — Doroshevich, (see note to page 108); Vasily Rozanov (1856-1919), critic, philosopher, iconoclast; Alexander Blok (1880-1921), major Symbolist poet.

p.151 Lydia Charskaya — a popular author of sentimental love stories in the 1920s.

p.153 *Alexei Tolstoy* — Count Aleksei KonstantinovichTolstoy (1817-1875), poet, playwright, author of the historical novel *Prince Serebryany* (1862).

p.153 Vera Zasulich (1849-1919), a Populist, later a Social Democrat; in 1878 tried to assassinate St. Petersburg governor F.F. Trepov. Acquitted by jury.

p.153 *the Lena River massacre* — More than 500 protest demonstrators (April 1912) were shot or wounded at the Lena gold mines in Siberia.

p.155 *in February of '17* — In February 1917 the monarchy was overthrown: Tsar Nicholas II abdicated, power passed to the Provisional Government.

p.156 *Muir & Merrilees* — an elegant department store (founded in the 1890s) next to the Bolshoi Theater.

p.157 Astrakhan, a city on the Volga where it joins the Caspian Sea; the area was famous for its ample fruit, vegetables and fish.

p.157 *"Like Epikhodov, he was a walking disaster"* — The clerk in Chekhov's play *The Cherry Orchard* (1903).

p.157 *quiet Akhtuba* — A town (later absorbed by Akhtubinsk) on the Akhtuba River flowing into the Caspian.

p158. *Spanish influenza* — The 1918-19 epidemic seized all of Europe; in Russia it coincided with the Civil War, hunger, cold and typhoid.

p.158 *Saratov* — a city on the Lower Volga.

p.159 *the labor front* — During the Civil War, many of those who were not drafted (e.g. women, boys, students) were assigned to dig trenches, build fortifications, rebuild railroads, etc.

p.160   *guitars — not yet branded as petty-bourgeois* — In the '20s, the guitar was associated with a petty-bourgeois way of life.

p.161   *Back then [this award] came without any royal insignia or privileges* — As of 1938, the Hero of Socialist Labor came with the coveted Order of Lenin and a Gold Star as well as many privileges.

p.162   *"Nothin' but Jews!"* — After the Revolution, with the abolition of the Jewish Pale, the influx of Jews to big cities and universities previously closed to them increased.

p.163   Boris Savinkov (1879-1925), theoretician of terrorism, leader of an anti-Soviet conspiracy.

p.165   *Vampuka* — an opera spoof (1909).

p.165   *NEP-era* — A temporary tactical retreat following War Communism, the New Economic Policy (introduced in 1921) allowed state-controlled private enterprise in trade, agriculture and industry.

p.167   *The Lower Depths* — a play (1902) by Maksim Gorky (1868-1936) depicting derelicts in a flophouse.

p.168   *later... fell in with the Industrial Party* — The "Industrial Party" (1926-30) was an invented underground organization, supposedly foreign-backed, bent on sabotage, espionage, etc. Thousands of people were arrested for involvement; at the open trial (1930), the party's eight "organizers" dutifully confessed to all manner of absurd crimes.

p.169   *Mashkov and Konchalovsky* — Ilya Mashkov (1881-1944) and Pyotr Konchalovsky (1876-1956): artists of the Russian avant-garde, founders of the Jack of Diamonds group.

p.169   *Sokolov-Skalya* — Pavel Sokolov-Skalya (1899-1961), student of Mashkov's turned painter of Soviet propaganda posters and scenes from Soviet history.

p.170   *Persimfans* — the first symphony orchestra with no conductor (1922-1932).

p.174   Nikolai Bukharin (1888-1938), Communist Party leader, editor of the *Pravda*. Executed as an "enemy of the people".

p.174   *Lion Feuchtwanger* — German author of historical novels (1884-1958); wrote glowingly of his 1937 visit to Moscow and of Stalin in his book *Moscow, 1937*.

p.174 *How the Steel Was Tempered* — a partially autobiographical novel (1932-34) by Nikolai Ostrovsky (1904-36) featuring a staunch Communist; both the author and the hero became part of the Soviet pantheon.

p.175 *Schutzbund* — a defense alliance of Austrian Social-Democrats (1923-34); their armed revolt was suppressed in Vienna (1934); of those Schutzbund members who made their way to the USSR, many later died in camp.

p.176 *Dzhugashvili* — Stalin's real (Georgian) last name.

p.177 *The Suicide*, a black comedy by Nikolai Erdman (1902-70), was staged but banned for publication. Erdman was exiled in 1934 while a film based on his script, *Merry Lads*, became Stalin's favorite.

p.178 Vasily Surikov (1848-1916), artist; known for his scenes from Russian history.

p.178 Lubov Orlova (1902-75), Hollywoodesque movie star in the '30s and '40s.

p.180 Roman Malinovsky (1876-1918), a ranking Bolshevik, later exposed as a tsarist police spy; fled Russia in 1914; shot on his return in 1918.

p.181 *nicknamed me OstapBender* — After the witty rogue Ostap Bender, hero of Ilf and Petrov's satirical novels *Twelve Chairs* (1928) and *The Golden Calf* (1931).

p.185 *The Great Opposition* (1941-47) by Lev Kassil (1905-70); *Old Man Khottabych* (1938) by Lazar Lagin (1903-79); *Wild Dog Dingo* (1939) by Ruvim Fraerman (1891-1972); *A Military Secret* (1935) by Arkady Gaidar (see note to page 41); *The School in the Forest* (1941) by E. Smirnova.

p.186 *Chapayev [was a good picture]. I liked the psychological attack* — Meaning the scene in which several rows of White-guard officers (the remains of the Kappel Army) stride smartly towards the enemy as if on parade.

p.187 *ratatouille soup* — in Russia, a rough-and-ready soup of whatever one had on hand.

p.187 *Timur and His Team* — In Gaidar's novel the good boy Timur and his friends help the elderly and the weak (see note to page 40).

p.187 Belye Stolby Clinic, an old psychiatric clinic near Moscow.

p.190 Nikolai Virta (1906-1976), official Soviet writer.

p.192 "The Lofty Malady", translated by George Reavey (The Poetry of Boris Pasternak, NY, Putnam, 1959).

p.194 Leonid Chertkov (1933-2000), leader of the first underground poetry group in the post-Stalin times, of which Andrei Sergeev was also a member.

p.195 *"I thought so! Chkalov's widow is going to marry Belyakov"* — See note to page 15.

p.197 *the Socialist-Revolutionary Fanny Kaplan* — Lenin's failed assassin, Kaplan wounded Lenin in the chest and neck in 1918 (her bullets became the pretext for the Red Terror); executed.

p.197 *"that Stalin ... had shot his wife"...Alliluyeva* — Stalin's wife, Nadezhda Alliluyeva (1901-1932), worked at the Council of People's Commissars and on the journal *Revolution and Culture*. She apparently committed suicide.

p.197 Anatoly Lunacharsky (1875-1933), Minister of Education (1917-29).

p.197 Aleksei Rykov (1881-1938), chairman of the Council of People's Commissars (1924-30). Rykov ordered vodka to be watered down to twenty-eight proof; this new, weaker vodka became known as *Rykovka*.

p.197 *A rumor... "that Meyerhold killed his wife, Zinaida Raikh, with an axe"*— Vsevolod Meyerhold (1874-1940), stage director, famous for his innovative ideas and productions; his theater was shut down in 1938; he was arrested in 1939 and soon shot; his wife, the actress Zinaida Raikh (1894-1939), was found savagely murdered in her apartment.

p.197 Vera Kholodnaya, star of the silent screen (1893-1919).

p.198 *"that all the obscene verses were composed by ... Sergei Esenin*— certain poems by Sergei Esenin (1895-1925) were picked up, recited and sung by the urban lower and criminal classes.

p.198 *From there it was just a step to killer-doctors*— In January 1953, a group of mainly Jewish doctors was arrested on charges of plotting to kill Soviet leaders. This anti-Semitic campaign would have led to the deportation of Jews if not for Stalin's death on 5 March 1953.

p.199 Maksim Litvinov (1876-1951), People's Commissar of Foreign Affairs (1930-39); removed from this post by Stalin during negotiations with Hitler at which point Litvinov's being a Jew became an inconvenience; reinstated in 1941 as ambassador to the United States.

p.199 *the Beiliss Affair* — A Jewish clerk in Kiev, Mendel Beiliss stood falsely accused (1911-13) of the "ritual murder" of a Russian boy; his trial provoked public outrage at home and abroad; acquitted by jury.

p.201 *Stalin drank to the Russian people* — Stalin's toast marked the beginning of a far-reaching campaign against "cosmopolitanism", a euphemism for all things Jewish and/or Western, from French pastry to Jewish doctors (see note to page 199).

p.201 *remembered the Tatars from that very time* — from the time of the Tatar-Mongol Yoke in Russia (1243-1480).

p.203 *the executioner Latvians* — In the 1930s, the security organs employed many Latvians, members of the Latvian Rifle Brigade (formed in 1915, it split into Red and White divisions after the Revolution). In the late '30s, these riflemen, Latvians or not, themselves became victims of the NKVD.

p.203 *They lumped Armenians together with Assyrians* — Assyrians were noticeable in Moscow where so many of them worked in little sidewalk booths shining shoes.

p.204 *"The Persians beat Griboyedov to death"* — Alexander Griboyedov (1795-1829), dramatist and diplomat; served as Russian minister to Persia where he was murdered when an angry mob attacked the Russian embassy in Teheran.